the
great
commandment

"You shall love the Sovereign your God with all your heart, and with all your soul, and with all your strength, and with all your mind; and your neighbor as yourself." "You shall love the Sovereign your God with all your heart, and with all your soul, and with all your strength, and with all your mind; and your neighbor as yourself." "You shall love the Sovereign your God with all your heart, and with all your soul, and with all your strength, and with all your mind; and your neighbor as yourself." "You shall love the Sovereign your God with all your heart, and with all your soul, and with all your strength, and with all your mind; and your neighbor as yourself." "You shall love the Sovereign your God with all your heart, and with all your soul, and with all your strength, and with all your mind; and your neighbor as yourself." "You shall love the Sovereign your God with all your heart, and with all your soul, and with all your strength, and with all your mind; and your neighbor as yourself." "You shall love the Sovereign your God with all your heart, and with all your soul, and with all your strength, and with all your mind; and your neighbor as yourself."

a theology

of resistance

and

transformation

ELEANOR H. HANEY

the great commandment

THE PILGRIM PRESS
CLEVELAND, OHIO

The Pilgrim Press, Cleveland, Ohio 44115

© 1998 by Eleanor H. Haney

Words and tune by Brigit McCallum © 1986. Used by permission.
Music and lyrics by Susan Savell, Freeport, Maine,
© Ritual Music, 1986. Used by permission of the author. Joan
Parrish's unpublished notes used by permission of the author.

Biblical quotations are from the New Revised Standard Version of
the Bible, © 1989 by the Division of Christian Education of the
National Council of the Churches of Christ in the U.S.A., and are
used by permission.

We have made every effort to trace copyrights on the materials
included in this publication. If any copyrighted material has
nevertheless been included without permission and due
acknowledgment, proper credit will be inserted in future printings
after receipt of notice.

Printed in the United States of America on acid-free paper

03 02 01 00 99 98   5 4 3 2 1

Library of Congress Cataloging-in-Publication Data
Haney, Eleanor Humes.
    The great commandment : a theology of resistance and
transformation / Eleanor H. Haney.
        p.   cm.
    Includes bibliographical references and index.
    ISBN 0-8298-1245-8 (alk. paper)
    1. Christianity and justice.   2. Feminist theology.
    3. Christian ethics.   4. Sociology, Christian.   I. Title.
BR115.J8   1998   IN PROCESS
261.8—dc21   97-46833
                                            CIP

TO

RACHEL HENDERLITE

1905-1991
LOVER OF GOD, LOVER OF JUSTICE

CONTENTS

Introduction: Commitments to Share and Act 1

1. Communities of Resistance and Nurture 18

2. Methods of Conversation and Commitment 37

3. Theology of God and the World 53

4. Ethics of Creation and New Creation 72

5. Transforming Life in the World. 106

Notes. 132

Selected Bibliography. 136

Index. 138

INTRODUCTION: COMMITMENTS TO SHARE AND ACT

We must use what we have to invent what we desire.
—*Adrienne Rich,* What Is Found There

For I am about to create new heavens and a new earth.
—*Isaiah 65:17a*

Increasingly, I have come to understand that white middle-class Christian feminist theology and ethics should be grounded in Christian communities and collective justice action sustained through the alliances we build with one another. In this book, therefore, I have started to develop such a theology and ethics. I offer it as a contribution to ongoing conversations and struggles about how Christians committed to justice "do" theology and ethics.

This positioning of white Christian feminist theology and ethics is the result of four convictions I have come to through my own involvement in justice work, my years of struggle with the church, and my ever-deepening awareness of the depths of oppression:

1. As a white middle-class Christian feminist, I can do only white middle-class Christian feminist theology and ethics. My experience and perspectives, though limited, can nevertheless contribute to a larger, rainbow-hued understanding of justice, theology, and ethics.
2. I understand justice to include earth as well as people, and I believe that social and ecological justice is central to God's activity in the world. *Salvation, redemption,* or *new creation* are images that point to powers in the world creating with us respectful relationships, patterns of shared power, and generous access to the richness of God's world for all creatures. Thus resistance to injustice and bearing wit-

ness to the possibilities of transformation are essential marks of the white church.

3. Feminist theology and ethics should be grounded in and guide the life and work of congregations. They should be rooted in worship and action, reflective of and guiding our experience of God, injustice, and the struggles for justice. And I believe that the contributions of feminists and other justice-seeking people are necessary if the church is to survive as one of the few institutions in this society with a mandate for justice.

4. Feminist theology and ethics should be grounded in congregational alliances with other justice-seeking congregations, individuals, and organizations in and outside the church. Alliances are sustained commitments among groups and individuals to share experiences and insights, pain and rage, dreams and fears, and to engage in collective action for justice. Alliances create a larger power base for action than individual groups can offer. They also enable white middle-class church members to hear the experiences of the oppressed. In forming these alliances, we white people find that whereas before our gaze was on black people or poor people, we now turn inward to ask ourselves, as white and/or middle-class: Who are we, and how have we benefited from the disenfranchisement of others? Then we can ask, What must *we* do to challenge such unjust patterns?

In this introduction, therefore, I want first to trace something of my own journey toward these convictions and the resultant theology and ethics. I will then elaborate briefly on each of the four convictions and will relate each to the major theological and ethical themes of the book. I will conclude with a brief overview of each chapter.

MY OWN JOURNEY

I grew up in a Presbyterian church in a small segregated town in Delaware. Its members were white, and although my childhood spanned the 1930s, I recall few signs of the Great Depression among the congregation. They were doctors, merchants, some farmers, teachers, postal workers—and their wives and children. I grew up with Robert Schumann's "Traümerei" for Sunday school music, solid Presbyterian hymns (no gospel or "old-time religion" music), intellectual sermons based on Presbyterian orthodoxy, and a biblical fundamentalism that was taken for granted but not really pushed.

As a young adult in Richmond, Virginia, in the 1950s, I became active at Eastminster, a Presbyterian mission church in the ghetto. In the midst of all the violence of racism, poverty, and despair that existed there, the church helped to make a difference in people's lives. I was able to share something of the congregation's struggles, and words such as "faith," "love," "justice," and "vocation" began to weave an indelible, richly textured pattern of meaning and authority around my heart and in my mind. In return, I found an acceptance and a purpose that had been missing for much of my life.

Later, I became a member of the Lutheran Church (ALC) for several years while I was teaching in the Midwest. I was not at home there. I did not appreciate its liturgical focus, I disagreed with its Christocentrism and law-and-gospel theology, I objected to its evangelical pietism, and I challenged its conservative individualistic ethics.

My experience with Lutheranism was a disaster, but it did inform me about how thoroughly I had been shaped by Reformed traditions, and when I returned to the East Coast, I eventually became a member of a congregation in the United Church of Christ (UCC). There is much that I love about the UCC, but I also continue to struggle with what I feel are its unjust patterns of worship, theology, and action. Nevertheless, for the time being, I find space within the UCC for the struggle.

This spiritual-ethical journey has been intrinsic to a more political one. In 1954, as the white South began to organize in opposition to the Supreme Court's mandate to end segregation in public schools, I arrived in Richmond to work in the newspaper "morgue"—the library. The town where I had grown up had been segregated, and the college I had attended had been all white. I did not question that pattern in either place. But the violence of the white response and the growing civil rights movement awakened me. I not only began worshiping and volunteering at Eastminster Church but also joined the faculty of Virginia Union University, an African American university in Richmond. Inevitably and willingly, I plunged into local civil rights activities. I worked primarily with colleagues and students from the university and with black ministers in the area, along with a few white people, including Rachel Henderlite, to whom this book is dedicated.[1] We registered black voters, demonstrated at, boycotted, and finally integrated major department stores, helped a black Presbyterian minister win the first black seat on the city council, and organized small integrated concerts and other arts events.

Later, while teaching in Minnesota, I became active in the movements of the 1960s—particularly the peace and environmental movements and, most significantly, the feminist movement. I worked with students on issues of the draft. I protested the U.S. involvement in Southeast Asia and nuclear weapons policy and production. I helped establish an environmental studies program at the college. And I experienced a profound metamorphosis as I came to grips with the reality of women's oppression and my own struggle to find and/or create a new identity and self-worth. Again I protested and boycotted; I also helped to establish a women's center in the area and to initiate women's studies courses. At the same time, I continued to challenge racism. I volunteered at the Fargo-Moorhead Indian Center and helped to establish the first public and multiracial day-care center in the area.

Since coming to Maine, I have helped to found the Feminist Spiritual Community, the Center for Vision and Policy, and the Maine Community Loan Fund recently combined with another loan fund to become the Genesis Community Loan Fund. The Feminist Spiritual Community cuts through barriers of class, age, and sexual preference to bring women together. Each week, members gather to share stories, create rituals, and open themselves to the spiritual dimensions of their lives. At the Center for Vision and Policy, I have spent nearly ten years learning to be in solidarity with white men, on the one hand, and with women and men of color, on the other, particularly indigenous women and men. The Genesis Community Loan Fund accepts investments from those who have and lends at very low interest rates to those who have not. Much of the funding supports affordable-housing endeavors, but some is used to assist small community-based, cooperatively run, and ecologically responsible businesses.

I have also been deeply involved with WINGS (Women in Nurturing Group Support), an organization of "working poor" and AFDC (Aid to Families with Dependent Children) women, particularly in the effort to buy land and build a community of affordable housing. And as a member of the Bath, Maine, UCC church, I have been working with United Voice, an organization that began as an AFDC support group sponsored by the local community-action agency. Since a major need in the midcoast Maine area is reliable private transportation (there is only occasional public transport), church and United Voice members began to hold bean suppers to raise money for car repairs, insurance, and auto club memberships. More recently, the United Voice women have formed a community land trust to provide permanent affordable homes for very low income families. They also work with and challenge the state legislature on issues of economic justice.

In feminism, I discovered the missing link, so to speak, that connects what had been separate and parallel in my life. Identifying patriarchy supplied the missing piece of my social reality and commitment to justice. Naming it helped to make sense of the whole.

In feminism, I also found a home, and I wept with the power of recognition. After all of the years of feeling that something was wrong with me, of feeling some-how isolated from the rest of the human community, I now began to understand that such feelings were the result of forces that were shaping my life and not of some deep fault within me. And I began to move into the center of my own existence.

As I claimed myself, I also experienced another truth. I found that I too belonged to this earth; I had a right to be and to walk on it. This grounding was equally and simultaneously a spiritual and a physical one. One summer while visit-ing my parents in Delaware with my young son, I took him crabbing in the bay. The early morning was still and bright; the blue water, white sand, and green dune grass were vivid in the warm, soft air. I glanced at my son, standing a few yards away, his crab line stretching out into the water. I felt a tug on my own line as a crab began to nibble the fish head on the end of the line. And I thought, "bone of my bone, flesh of my flesh": my flesh made in part from years of eating crabs, David's flesh made from my flesh and his father's, the crab's flesh made from scraps of everything that fell to the bottom of the water, the sun warming and transforming all—crab, boy, woman, grass, sand, and water. We are indeed one flesh.

Feminism has been absolutely critical for me. Yet in retrospect, I believe that the racial-justice movement of the 1950s and early 1960s, along with my experience of God—mediated in part through the church—has been more radicalizing for me than feminism has been. The former was the occasion and condition of a personal coming to vocation and meaning—to a unity and direction of self. It brought together spirituality and ethics, or politics; it set the path for my life. Feminism built on this base; it gave me analytical tools to understand the interrelations and contradictions of oppression, and it gave me the ability to affirm myself. As I encountered the feminist movement, I said to myself, "Oh, yes, I too belong; I too am valued and worth fighting for." Through feminism, I reached *a* turning point in a journey. In the racial-justice movement, I embarked on *the* journey, from which there was no turning back.

Although the metaphor of journey is helpful for imagining one's growing and changing, life is not a road. It is too multidirectional; one explores many roads simultaneously, and they all crisscross, weaving in and out of one another. So as I was pursuing the journeys described above, I was also discovering and celebrating, with other women, relationships of intimacy, respect, and friendship of a depth that I had not experienced with men. Of course, these experiences have led to connecting heterosexist oppression to other oppressions. Further, I am now working on issues of injustice and justice with women who have managed to survive mental health systems. I am embarking on redefining what it means—and could mean—to grow old as a white woman in this society. And the focus of both my action and my reflection has become increasingly centered on economic issues. A fundamental condition of justice in every area of life is economic power and sufficiency.

These, then, are some of the experiences that have brought me to writing the theology and ethics in this book. They have brought me a clearer understanding of what I can and cannot do; they have brought me back to the church, to an ever-deepening sense of injustice and commitment to justice and to the necessity of alliance-building.

ECOSOCIAL LOCATION

If I have learned anything from my life, it is that as a theologian, ethicist, and activist, I have a limited understanding, one relative to who I am and the institutions and cultures that have shaped me. To pretend to more absolute or universal insights and truths is to perpetuate the oppression my life is committed to challenging.

I have coined the term "ecosocial location" to help analyze this social/personal reality. We are shaped by our participation in racial-ethnic, gender, sexual-orientation, age, national, ability, and biological groups and geographical settings. I am white, of northern European ancestry and culture, female, academically trained with a Ph.D., in a lesbian relationship, a member of a largely white and middle-class Protestant denomination, from a lower-middle-class background, sixty-five years old, a representative of the culture's understanding of mental and emotional normalcy, physically able-bodied, and an easterner who deeply loves the ocean.

These groupings are not natural; they are constructed. They have been given meanings and values by a dominant group and its culture. For instance, as a white woman in this culture, I have had a value that not only differed from that of an African American woman but also was superior in the eyes of the dominant culture. So, theoretically, I am to be protected in a way not afforded to black women. (I can also be raped, of course, but the dominant culture has said that only white—not black—men can rape me with impunity.)

Yet I am not shaped only by the dominant culture, however determinative. I also respond and, in doing so, can draw on more sources than are "officially" given to me. I have come to value my racial and gendered history in ways quite different from those I learned in school. I have struggled to reinterpret my racial history in light of its heritage of mammoth injustice, I have had to unearth and hold close my women's heritage, and I have had to re-create both meaning and value in my white women's history. As a member of a feminist spiritual community, I help uncover and even create new meanings and values. So I am not only shaped; to however small an extent, I am also a shaper.

Social group membership and its meanings and values are not the only component of ecosocial location. We are located institutionally, with roles, positions, and degrees and with social power and unearned advantages. By and large, white males have had the power to determine who has access to food, shelter, education, positions of leadership, health care, and other resources in this country. Underlying these powers has been their power to name the world, to name reality, in light of their experiences and interests. But white middle-class and/or professional women also have been given certain unearned advantages and power—as well as denied them. Peggy McIntosh and others have described many of the ways in which we have such advantages and power.[2]

In addition to unearned advantages and power, many white women, as well as men, have positions of earned power and advantage, positions that are part of our ecosocial location. These demand analysis and careful consideration about how they can be used to challenge oppression. Otherwise, they—and thus we—simply further oppression. Many white women work in social service agencies, for instance, as case-workers and managers. The clients—women who are poor, disabled, ill—all too often share experiences of appalling treatment by the women in positions of power over them. Sometimes, of course, they experience outright hostility and prejudice. Often, however, dominance is experienced more subtly. One way is by the exercise of the privilege of charity. Women social workers dispense vouchers, money, apart-ments, and financial aid; they expect the *others* to be compliant and grateful. If an *other* refuses to be an object of charity and becomes a subject, an *I*, the social worker's smile becomes a frown, and if the "gift" must still be given, it is done so begrudgingly and even angrily. A friend of mine, who is "on welfare," had to have an MRI. The nurse was friendly until my friend suggested a change in the procedure because of her medical condition, a suggestion that was apparently perceived as ques-tioning the nurse's expertise. Charity abruptly ended, and as the examination contin-ued, the nurse belittled my friend and muttered about people "abusing the system."

A second way that dominance is often displayed is through innocence. Many white women have the luxury (an unearned advantage) of innocence, which they bring with them into their roles. They/we are sincere and well-intentioned but blind. And we simply don't—and don't really try to—understand why our "clients" get sullen, uncooperative, or angry or become troublemakers. It is not only corpo-rate heads who can ignore the life realities of people who are oppressed but also those of us, generally white women, who are in daily contact with people "below" us. We are sincerely committed to justice for all, but our innocence subverts us, and we actually reinforce the status quo.

Finally, the concept of ecosocial location points to the ways that we are shaped by the natural world of which we are a part and, conversely, the ways that we give it certain meaning, value, power, and advantage. I live in a body that structures my existence in multiple ways; the dominant culture has also specified how my body is supposed to structure me; and I have come to reconstruct how I understand my body and have thus altered the way it structures me! Similarly, I have lived near the Atlantic Ocean most of my life, and its images, smells, and power are richly woven in me. At the same time, both the dominant culture and I assign certain meanings and values to the ocean. To some extent, these meanings are quite different.

For theology and ethics, the implications of our existence as ecosocially located are many and profound. One is that we must ground our abstractions in real pat-terns of relationships and specifically recognize that these patterns are part of struc-tures of unjust power and oppressive assignment of meaning and value to the diversity of human groups and the natural world. It is not enough to say that we are relational beings or that we are interdependent, both current concepts in construct-ing theologies of selfhood. We are those, but our relationships, our interdependen-cies, are patterned in ways that do violence—perhaps finally to all of us, but more immediately and surely to most of us and to the natural world. To say that we are interdependent is to gloss over and mask the very real discrepancies of power in the world and the oppression, violence, and unearned, radically unequal privilege that goes with that power.

Further, as an ethicist, I must be clear about how I participate in and perpetuate those patterns. I must bring a hermeneutic of suspicion to the theology and ethics *I* seek to do. Womanist theologians continue to challenge white feminist theologians precisely at this point, and we join in challenging white and sometimes black male theologians here. For instance, Delores Williams wrote: "Though many white feminists speak of multilayered oppression . . . , they do not give serious attention to the ways they participate in and help perpetuate the terrible social and cultural value systems that oppress all black people. Very few if any discussions of patriarchy give full and serious attention to women's oppression of women."[3]

CONGREGATIONS AS SOURCES FOR FEMINIST THEOLOGY AND ETHICS

I am increasingly coming to understand how critical it is to claim a space within the church and to accept some responsibility for shaping its future. Since I am a member of a Christian community, my theological and ethical reflection is grounded in my experience of those powers I name "God" and also in a community's experiences—in worship, action, and mutual support. Such experiences deepen, challenge, and correct my own experiences, even as mine can do the same for others in the congregation. My experience is also, of course, grounded in ecospecific social locations of others in the congregation, which may be quite diverse and complex or more uniform. Where there is the richness of diversity, there are many opportunities for alliances within the community as well as between this community and others.

The expression of the church that has been significant for me is part of what sociologists call "mainline churches." These are the Protestant churches that have been closely related to the white European American dominant culture. These are the churches that have nurtured, challenged, and appalled me. They have stereotyped me, accepted me, and rejected me. These are the churches of the denominations that, as many analysts have pointed out, have been losing membership, financial support, and social and political influence.[4] Increasing secularization, the growth of the Christian Right, and the growth of Islamic, Eastern, and New Age forms of religion have all challenged the hegemony of mainline Protestantism.

These are troubled churches, many of them struggling to survive. It is to a congregation within them that I have returned. Why? Why is it so important to me to work within such congregations? In and through my working with and founding justice organizations, I have deeply, passionately longed for a community in which to celebrate the power(s) of the universe I have learned to name God and to work on issues of justice and new creation. I have longed for a community that speaks a biblical as well as feminist language, that shares a vision and a vocation, that nurtures and challenges me, that shares resistance to injustice. Further, and perhaps more important, the church is one of few communities, and the only one I am familiar with, that is rooted in the experience and affirmation of the eternal power in the universe that seeks our well-being and the well-being of all creatures and that has a mission to witness to that power. At its best, the church even incarnates dimensions of the love and justice expressed in the life of Jesus. It is vitally important to maintain an institutional expression of that experience and mission, particularly now as the Christian Right seeks to monopolize the term "Christian" and give it a somewhat different and, for me, unjust meaning.

And so I have returned to the church to work within it. There are always people in the church with justice visions and longings and commitments, a remnant, if you will. I believe that it may be possible to connect with remnants and contribute my feminist analyses, commitments, and experiences of alliance-building to establish an exciting and experimental prophetic ministry of celebration, support, and action. The congregations that become a part of this ministry will be in many ways in opposition to the dominant culture; they will be churches of a post-Christendom, or post-Constantinian, era. I am convinced that they will be more faithful to the God revealed in Jesus.

This book begins, therefore, with the church, with a congregation committed to justice and new creation. It is a congregation similar to the one I am a member of, a congregation in a "mainline" church. It is in the process of finding its prophetic voice.

What might this congregation look like? What kind of alliances has it formed? What is its worship like? How does it maintain community? What is its institutional shape? In answering these questions, I envision a congregation that is part reality and part possibility. Many congregations already reflect some of the structures and practices I describe. Others are certainly possible. Many are illustrative or suggestive; they are designed to evoke the readers' ideas and actions appropriate to their own churches.

The congregation I describe, for instance, understands worship as communion—as being in the presence of God, delighting in God, deepening its relationship with God, and gaining strength and direction for the work of justice and bearing witness to new creation. It images God as powers beyond any or all of us but also intimately present in the community. So worship is very much a communal activity, with opportunities to share and hear pain, grief, joy, struggle. The language of worship also seeks to reflect the whole of the community and its diverse understanding of God. To facilitate a communal experience, this congregation sold the sanctuary pews and replaced them with chairs and even a few large cushions.

The congregation is learning how to address racism, patriarchy, and other forms of oppression within itself and the larger church and society. It has also made a commitment to work toward creating more just, local economic alternatives.

The congregation relies largely on lay leadership; in fact, it has stopped using the categories of "professional" and "lay." It does support several part-time resource and staff people, including one with theological and ministerial training. It inherited a building, but it shares space with another congregation. It also makes space available to many community groups. Its budget for staff and maintenance is much lower than previously, and although its total budget—and size of its congregation—is smaller than formerly, the percentage of its funds for outreach has significantly grown.

JUSTICE ACTION AS A SOURCE FOR FEMINIST THEOLOGY AND ETHICS

Feminist theology and ethics are grounded in a commitment to justice. The definition of "justice" that I work with in this book includes more equally shared power, shared access to society's resources, and social as well as personal respect for the diversity and integrity of human and nonhuman life. Justice is thus political, economic, and cultural. Increasingly I believe that at its heart, justice is social power, shared equally—or more equally—and ultimately shared cosmically. This belief has profound implications for how we think about God, as well as about human, interspecies, and human-earth relationships. At the heart of this book, therefore, is the exploration of both the theoretical and the practical significance of shared power.

Grounding ethics in justice work has wide-ranging significance. White feminists have had to learn, sometimes painfully, that justice for women must be embraced in a larger, more complex commitment to racial justice and economic justice, to sexual justice, to justice for people outside the United States, to justice for all the creatures of the earth and for the earth itself. A part of the ethical task is, therefore, to try to understand how all the structures of injustice are related to one another, what justice might mean in different contexts, and how we can work on specific issues in relation to a larger whole.

This is impossible to do with any certainty, of course. The causes I am a part of are necessarily concrete and limited if I am to be of any real use, but I should be knowledgeable of others and sensitive to the ways that different causes can and do affect one another. Nor do I have any real expectation that there is some underlying harmonious relationship even if we cannot see it. The world is so broken, the history of oppression so pervasive and long-standing, that there will be contradictory claims of justice. Difficult, agonizing, preferential choices have to be made, but we still have to be responsive to these conflicts—not ignore them.

The grounding of theology and ethics in justice means that theology and ethics are measured by the extent to which they reflect, promote, and/or deny justice. To what extent do my doctrines of God, of the self, and of ethics reflect racism or my own internalized sexism or homophobia?

As I try to relate ecological and social justice, one of the tasks I identify is the need for a new, nonoppressive construction of the natural world. We must begin to sort through the various Western constructions of the natural world, specifically two of the dominant ones: a Darwinian, Victorian, patriarchal, racist construct; and the "Thoreauian" reaction to the industrial revolution, a romantic construct. White feminists have too unsuspiciously created our own construction, largely indebted to a romantic one. We also must listen to the ways other groups have constructed the natural world—particularly African American and indigenous peoples. Little specific writing about the natural world can yet be found in womanist literature, except for the image of wilderness (which is quite different from an indigenous image), although careful examination of the black slavery, sharecropping, and farming traditions in this country would probably result in another unique construction.[5]

And somehow we must find ways to open ourselves to the voices of birds and animals and plants, to put ourselves in just relationships with them, even as we try both to image and to determine what such relationships might be.

ALLIANCE WORK: COVENANTING FOR JUSTICE AND TRANSFORMATION

As a white feminist Christian, I must be in communication and commitment—in alliance—with those whose experiences of and perspectives on injustice and justice are significantly different from mine. Working in alliances is similar to what liberation theologians call "standing in solidarity." It is committing oneself or a community to enter into sustained conversation with, support of, and collective action for people—particularly activists—of diverse racial-ethnic cultures, classes, ages, sexual identities, abilities, and genders.

Alliances have special characteristics: they demand commitment; they begin to break down the dividing walls of hostility by forcing participants to address inequalities of power and unearned social advantages and to work through stereotyping and suspicion toward honesty and trust; they create a broader and more coherent challenge to oppression and violence; and they set the context and condition for faithful theological and ethical reflection.

MAKING COMMITMENTS

Alliances demand commitment. Initially, at least, and perhaps for an extended period, the commitment may be unilateral, for it is a commitment by those with some social power and unearned privilege to those with less. This is both a general commitment and a commitment to specific others. Generally it means that through reading and conversation, we learn of the perspectives, insights, and struggles of other people. Equally it means, as George Tinker has written, "self-reflection on one's own privileged status in the world and mov[ing] toward a commitment to relinquish that privileged status."[6] Entering into an alliance or helping to create one is making a covenant promise with oneself and others—to risk misunderstanding and being misunderstood, to stay with the others in the relationship, and to be open to challenge and transformation.

A congregation may covenant to be in alliance with women in our struggles for justice, for instance. One expression of that may be to work with abused women who gradually come to trust that the congregation is "there" for them. As that trust grows, the relationship becomes mutual.

Alliances are thus quite different from coalitions. Limited and specific, coalitions are formed out of mutual self-interest. An environmental organization might join with a business to oppose specific legislation seen as inimical to both. Once the situation no longer exists, the coalition dissolves and the two go their separate ways.

In alliances, a general commitment must be embodied, incarnate in specific commitments to specific others—to the local chapter of the NAACP, to a womanist caucus in a theological or ethical professional organization, to members of a Buddhist temple in the next town, to a support group of women on AFDC.

Maintaining this commitment involves a process that is long, difficult, frustrating, and rewarding. The alliance between members of the Center for Vision and Policy and certain indigenous people grew out of many long hours of conversation in which the indigenous people gradually assumed more and more leadership. Commitments were made slowly, only after some measure of trust was experienced by both sides, and yet of course, some commitments were also made very early. Natives and whites both had to be willing to put themselves at risk and make themselves vulnerable to one another at a very early stage. Without that kind of commitment, trust would not have had time to develop. So alliances are long-term, multipurpose relationships that acknowledge and value personal as well as functional dimensions of the relationship. Alliances provide a context for coming to know one another, for sharing dreams and fears as well as planning action.

We cannot make commitments of long-term common action with every group, but we have a responsibility to stay informed about women, men, and the earth wherever they are exploited, subjected to violence, or marginalized. Such communication should be firsthand—hearing or reading what women in Africa themselves have to say, for instance, rather than hearing or reading what someone else has to say about them.

BREAKING DOWN WALLS

In alliances, the inequalities of social power and privilege are identified and challenged. Those with power and unearned advantage—for instance, white feminist women—learn to listen and hear; we relinquish the power and privilege we bring to the relationship. We relinquish our own assumptions about and patterns of leadership and "getting things done."

This is often quite difficult to do. It is difficult to remain and listen; it is even more difficult to take others as partners in the work of justice rather than as "case studies" or "resources for information" or "objects of charity." It is one thing to *use* an AFDC woman's story as I figure out the "right" way to address issues of poverty. It is quite another to figure out the right way together.

Sometimes we can't do anything but stand by and wait. I think one of the hardest lessons I have learned is that we can't "fix" everything. We often can only "be there." And sometimes we can't even be there. I recall an election that was scheduled on a reserve where we were trying to support the work of a few people to establish a cultural resource center. One person was running for office against the opposition of the people in power on the reserve. According to our information, the elections would be fraudulent, and we volunteered to be there simply as witnesses. But we were told that our presence would only make things more difficult for our friends who had to live there, so we had to sit by and do nothing.

In the process of forcing us to identify and break down inequalities of power, alliances also enable us to begin to replace stereotyping with honesty and to replace mistrust, fear, and/or hostility with trust and vulnerability. Both parties have to work through layer upon layer of stereotypes—positive ones as well as negative, romantic as well as demeaning ones. Unfortunately, some white people bring to a potential alliance romantic stereotypes about indigenous people, become disillusioned, and withdraw rather than replace stereotypes with reality. They are unwilling to be honest about their own stereotyping or to allow native people to be themselves. If the white people had been willing to stay with their commitments, they could have become stronger in themselves, more in touch with the depth of the evils of oppression and the complexities of the human condition, as well as clearer about the urgency of the demands of justice.

To turn the relationship around, so to speak, and look at it from the other side, when we white feminist women form alliances with white men, for instance, we have other tasks. One is simply to come to trust that such a relationship is possible and desirable, a belief that is in part faith and in part conclusion. We must also be willing to hold men accountable for their sexism, and at least to some extent, we must be teachers about their political responsibilities and the risks of solidarity. We must insist on our own leadership, being gradually willing to share it. And we must be able to forgive—to allow sexist behavior as long as men are willing to learn, even as we commit racist actions and seek forgiveness and accountability in our dedication to alliances with people of color.

ACTING IN COHERENCE

In alliances, the partners not only turn toward one another but also stand together, facing the larger society. The more marginal partners in the alliance articulate goals and needs and work with the more privileged partners to determine where they justly fit into those goals and needs. Together they work out an action plan for change.

The more the partners have moved toward shared power, respect, and trust, the more analysis and plans for action are also shared. Those with social power and unearned advantages contribute their own role and insights into how the structures are maintained and how to use their "connections" for justice. But I doubt that it is possible yet to have a fully democratic process for determining the direction of resistance or change. Until there is genuinely shared power and deep respect and trust, those with less power must ultimately make decisions of policy, philosophy, and action.

Alliances also enable us to relate our own specific struggles to larger, ultimately global ones. As several of us whites work in alliance with indigenous people in Maine and New Brunswick, for instance, we are drawn into an international network of indigenous people struggling to survive, to preserve their cultures and regain power over their own futures. Our actions are set in this global context and are accountable to it. Further, as we work on other issues—an end to sexual harassment, for instance—our analyses, goals, and actions are also related to these other struggles. We have an opportunity to explore cross-cultural patterns and meanings around sexual activity, gestures, touch, and words; to become aware of alternative approaches and resources as we seek to reshape our own patterns; and even to challenge those with whom we are in alliance about dimensions of sexual harassment in their own cultures.

Finally, alliances underlie the development of faithful theology and ethics. I do not think that valid, accurate, true feminist theory, and specifically feminist theology, can be articulated in a narrowly circumscribed feminist context. Clearly a European American feminist context alone is insufficient, a middle-class context alone is insufficient, a heterosexual context alone is insufficient, an academic context alone is insufficient, a church context alone is insufficient—alone all are insufficient. Theology that is sensitive to the dimensions of privilege and the biases of ecosocial location, theology that is knowledgeable about perceptions and values and traditions and ways of being in the world by a diversity of people, is most likely to avoid the weaknesses and falsehoods of so much of traditional dominant theology. We must learn how to do theology that is rooted in the practice of alliance and is accountable to a diversity of peoples.

Delores Williams writes of the necessity of womanists and feminists to be in real conversation with each other if a genuinely better future for black communities is to be envisioned and worked toward: "We must, like Hagar, obtain through our God-given faith *new vision* to see survival and quality-of-life resources where we have seen none before. Since feminists and womanists come from many cultures and countries, womanist-feminist dialogue and action may well provide some of the necessary resources. Recognizing and honoring our differences and commonalties can lead in directions we can perhaps both own."[7] She offers the following invitation and challenge: "Can we trust each other enough to build a present and future life together instead of digging the grave for our separate futures?"[8]

I respond: "Yes, we must continue to learn to, and we can do that only in alliance. It can be very hard work, but it is also tremendously exciting and transformative!"

OUTLINE OF THE BOOK

As I wrote above, since the congregation is a major source of the feminist theology and ethics proposed in this book, as well as an important site for the work of alliance-building, chapter 1 begins with a proposed model for congregational life. It describes one example of a mainline congregation committed to justice and new creation. Chapter 1 answers the questions of how congregations of such churches can become sites of celebration, support, and resistance. How can they become communities in which we hear and respond to God's call to friendship and discipleship?

The rest of the book addresses issues of feminist theology and ethics as they arise out of alliances and work within congregations, as well as with other justice and feminist spirituality organizations. Chapter 2 considers a Christian feminist method rooted in alliance work, justice action, worship, and study. It explores the implications of these for how we do theology and ethics. A number of questions are addressed. One concerns the nature of theological truth. How might we construct an understanding of God that is going to be always in process, since our perspectives are diverse, limited, and changing, even when we extend the circle of perspectives through alliances? Further, if my insights and experiences are relative to my ecosocial location, can I say that something is true? Am I an authority? If I were to make that claim, am I repeating what white male theologians have done? Where does authority lie? A further, critical question for many of us concerns how we bring the resources in non-Christian feminist spirituality and goddess traditions into a Christian feminist understanding of God. And a central, underlying question concerns how we understand Jesus and the biblical witness as resources for feminist theology and ethics.

Chapters 3 through 5 move into substantive discussions of theology and ethics. In chapter 3, I delineate an understanding of God set into a construction of reality as relational. Then following a discussion of what I mean by "power," I explore certain characteristics or qualities of relationships that I name expressions of sacred power or powers. God is the power of growth, of survival, of solidarity, of liberation, of creativity. And God is mystery.

In chapter 4 I turn to a more in-depth look at God as creator, at ourselves as creatures in ecosystems, and at the relation between creation and new creation, within which I suggest some ways for thinking about sin and redemption.

In chapter 5, I offer a vision and some resources for moving toward a more just society. I suggest a way of understanding two classical ethical concerns—decision-making and "virtue"—from a feminist perspective, and I explore courage and respect specifically. Then I turn to an examination of the possibilities for economic justice in the theological context I have developed in the discussion of creation and new creation, and I delineate some principles of action in the area of economic-eco-logical justice.[9]

In both the methodological and the theological discussions, you will see a profound indebtedness to several people. Delores Williams and Susan Thistlethwaite are important to me primarily through their writings. Williams's *Sisters in the Wilderness: The Challenge of Womanist God-Talk* and Thistlethwaite's *Sex, Race, and God: Christian Feminism in Black and White* are two of the major foundations for this work.[10] *Sisters in the Wilderness* is one of those books that act like a lens adjuster on binoculars: it enables you to see clearly what before was blurred or what you thought maybe you had only imagined was there. *Sex, Race, and God* raises many of the questions that white feminists have to address.

Several other people have been significant, through our face-to-face conversations and our friendships. With Susan Davies and Marvin Ellison, professors at Bangor Theological Seminary, I have an ongoing discussion about the themes of this book. In addition, they both have carefully read the manuscript, made numerous suggestions, and raised many questions, to which I continue to respond.

A third person is David Hall, the former minister of the church to which I belong. We have continuing conversations about theology and ethics and, in partic-ular, the future of the church. Through his leadership, I have actually participated in a congregation's decision to initiate change that it trusts will enable it to respond faithfully to God as it moves into the future.

Debbie Leighton, my partner, and many friends and colleagues have also informed this book—through conversation, mutual action, and the quality of our lives together.

I have no doubt that I will be charged by some as a heretic for the theology I sketch in this book. I find it impossible to do feminist theology and not be a heretic. And I remind myself that truth and orthodoxy are not synonyms and that the God I trust and adore is "larger" than any system of beliefs, including mine.

In writing this book, I had at least three audiences in mind. The first is other white feminist women struggling with similar issues and their participation in the institutional church. We have our work to do in the struggle for justice and well-being, and I offer this to you as a step in the further clarification of that work and as a resource both to challenge and to nurture you.

The second audience is womanists and feminists of color. I offer this book as a paragraph in an ongoing conversation. I have tried to be knowledgeable of the issues and the possibilities among and between us, although my focus has been primarily on those between African American womanists and white feminists. This focus is due to the fact that I don't yet know how to write as concretely to a much wider diversity.

The third audience includes those women and men open to the issues and struggles recorded and/or addressed here. I have learned much from you, and I invite you to participate more deeply in a feminist process and struggle for justice and well-being.

This book has been many years in the making, and my exploration of its subject will continue after these pages are written. I bring to it what I have learned in struggle, pain, and joy about living and working for justice. I bring to it tremendous love for the powers I name God, and I bring to it anger at the continuing destruction of God's creation and the demonic patterns of thinking, valuing, and acting that enable people to justify the violence they do. I don't bring a lot of hope, but I bring an imperative: we must continue to act, regardless of how likely a more just and healthful society is. We are called to faithfulness, not to success or practicality.

Finally, that is all that matters.

COMMUNITIES OF RESISTANCE AND NURTURE

"You shall love the Sovereign your God with all your heart, and with all your soul, and with all your strength, and with all your mind; and your neighbor as yourself." "You shall love the Sovereign your God with all your heart, and with all your soul, and with all your strength, and with all your mind; and your neighbor as yourself."

Ho, everyone who thirsts,
　　come to the waters;
and you that have no money,
　　come, buy and eat!
Come, buy wine and milk
　　without money and without price. . . .
Listen carefully to me and eat what is good,
　　and delight yourselves in rich food.
Incline your ear and come to me;
　　listen so that you may live.

—Isaiah 55:1–3a

Keep simple ceremonies
Follow the quest
Bring crystals and flowers
　　to the sea mother's breast.
—Susan Savell, "Keep Simple Ceremonies"

With all our hearts, we long for relationships of mutual delight. With all our hearts, we long for relationships in which we belong—firmly, unconditionally. With all our hearts, we long for relationships that invite us to share in the generous richness of the earth. The tragedy of our lives, however, is that for the most part, our relationships are broken. They do violence to us; they are indifferent to us. At the same time, of course, some of us profit from such patterns, so much so that the relationships seem tolerable or even good, so much so that we even try to kill the small voice of pain within.

For many years, as I recounted in the introduction, I did not believe that the church could be a community in which the longings of our hearts could be met. More recently, I have come to understand that the church must be such a community. That is, I have come to understand that what we call "the church" can be an expression of that community. "The church" may or may not coincide with the body of people who gather to worship on Sunday and who plan and implement the programs of the institution. The Body of Christ exists wherever and whenever such a gathering is committed to being a community of celebration of the generous and limiting powers in the universe as our understanding of them has been shaped by Jesus; of the nurture, healing, and challenging of our hearts' deepest longings; of resistance to the obscenities of oppression and destruction of life on earth; and of witness to God's new creation. This chapter explores some of the ways in which community, struggling to reflect such faithfulness, might live out its commitments and organize its life.

A COMMUNITY MOVED AND MOVING AWAY
FROM THE CENTER

Within the next ten to twenty years, the mainline churches will be much less central to the dominant society than they are now, and that move has already begun. By "mainline" churches, I mean those of a European heritage whose membership has been largely white, of middle and upper strata, and whose leaders believed that when they spoke, people at the centers of government, business, and education listened. These are Protestant churches—Presbyterian, Methodist, Lutheran, United Church of Christ, and Disciples of Christ. They are losing their positions near the center of U.S. society for many reasons, three of which I will highlight below: the increased secularization of the dominant culture; the increased political significance of the Christian Right; and the prophetic heritage in churches' own faith commitments. Then I will briefly explore the significance for the church of the changing directions of the U.S. economy.

INCREASED SECULARIZATION

Over the past fifteen years, my students at the Maine College of Art have increasingly come from secular households. Their parents, they tell me, have given them no religious experience because the parents want the children "to make up their own minds." In a religion class I taught in the spring of 1994, out of a class of twenty students, at least half came from such backgrounds; a few were disaffected Catholics, and only one considered herself a Christian, as a result of a conversion experience.

Among my white friends and colleagues, I lead something of a split life. With a few exceptions, the people in my activist circles have been non-Christians and non-religious Jews. The exceptions are primarily Quakers and a few UCC people. A few of the others practice various forms of an earth-based spirituality. Most are simply secular. Many of the indigenous women and men I work with, however, live out of an integral spiritual-political framework. That is also true of the few African American women I am close to.

This pattern is not unique to Maine. *Time* reported that the UCC had lost 21 percent of its members between 1965 and 1989.[1] In his study of mainline churches, Loren Mead concluded that much of the decline was due to this secularization. It was "as if the church somehow slipped off their radar screen."[2]

POLITICAL POWER OF THE CHRISTIAN RIGHT

In contrast to the erosion of membership (and finances) in the mainline churches, other churches are growing. The growth ranges from 23 percent in the Catholic church to 183 percent in the Church of God. Some new churches, shaped by twelve-step programs and New Age spirituality themes, are also growing. Unity is one of the former. And an interest in individual, noninstitutionalized religion seems also to be growing, as evidenced by the popularity of books such as Scott Peck's *The Road Less Traveled.*

By far the major part of this growth is in the so-called Christian Right. These are churches that are generally grouped under the rubric "evangelical." But they form a diverse group. Their diversity is reflected in their understanding of the Bible, in their doctrine, and in their relation to U.S. society, or "the world." Some are fundamentalist, affirming the inerrancy of Scripture—accepting a literal interpretation unless a passage is obviously metaphorical—and its straightforward application to contemporary belief and practice. Some are charismatics, stressing the gifts of the Holy Spirit and occasionally remaining within the mainline denominations. Some are Pentecostals, also stressing the gifts of the Holy Spirit and giving less importance to doctrine and law. Some are former fundamentalists that have in fact modified that position, recognizing that the Bible also contains much that is culturally and historically relative. Some hold dimensions of the above but are actively engaged in social-justice work and may, on given issues, be consistent ethically with "leftist" mainline church positions.

Most evangelicals have been committed to sharing their spiritual experiences and trying to convert others. Until recently, most were also "otherworldly." Their priority was individual salvation and waiting for Christ to return to establish justice and peace. That priority has changed dramatically, however. As white evangelical members have become more affluent, they have also shifted from a concern with the next world to a passionate concern about this one.[3] According to a 1994 *New Yorker* article, in the 1992 presidential election, evangelical Protestants were the "single largest constituency within the Republican Party," displacing the dominance of mainline Protestant Republicans.[4]

The Christian Coalition has become the most-organized expression of the evangelical shift and passion. Its purpose is "to speak out against anti-Christian bigotry and to make [the U.S.] government more responsive to the concerns of Christians and pro-family Americans."[5] To achieve that goal, it provides Christian voters with information, represents Christians before governments, registers Christians to vote, and protests unfair treatment of Christians by media and government.

It holds grassroots training sessions for organizing and gaining control in the Republican Party in each state as well as on local, state, and national governing bodies, for example, school boards. It has "schools, institutes, newspapers, magazines, radio and television stations and thousands of politically motivated churches."[6] The result is that the Christian Coalition has become a political constituency in the Republican Party. From that position, members are challenging the traditional political party leaders who have been part of the dominant culture—the mainline Protestant Democrats and those Pat Robertson calls the "secular humanists."[7]

What are the Coalition's positions? Most of us are familiar with its anti-abortion and anti-gay-and lesbian-rights stands, as well as its efforts to cut back on welfare funds and to include "creationism science" in the public schools. Behind these positions are at least two major theological emphases. One is *dominion theology.* This is part of a postmillenial eschatology that holds that Christ will return after the world has become more righteous and that Christians are to rule the earth and make it just in preparation for Christ's return. Robertson has written: "There will never be world peace until God's house and God's people are given their rightful place of leadership at the top of the world. How can there be peace when drunkards, communists, atheists, New Age worshipers of Satan, secular humanists, oppressive dictators, greedy moneychangers, revolutionary assassins, adulterers, and homosexuals are on top?"[8] Dominion theology also holds that all biblical laws have validity for all people and all institutions. Another dominion theologian, Rousas John Rushdoony, wrote, "The death penalty [should] be enforced today for adulterers, homosexuals, blasphemers, astrologers, witches and teachers of false doctrine."[9]

Some other theologians, however, are seen as *constitutionalists.* They accept religious pluralism and do not believe that all biblical laws can be applied universally. Instead, they seek reform of legislation—making laws consistent with the Constitution, which they believe is deeply rooted in biblical law.

Another organization of the Christian Right that brings together religion and politics is the Institute for Religion and Democracy (IRD). According to a 1983 editorial in the *Christian Century,* the organization was founded in 1981 to seek "a church stance that . . . supports a Reagan foreign policy,"[10] presumably bringing the mainline churches more in accord with a free-market economy and an anti-Communist position. As part of that program, it sought to monitor Protestant church budgets and discredit mainline churches' social positions.[11] The IRD also set the framework for a *60 Minutes* television program on the National Council of Churches (NCC) in 1983; among other things, the NCC was accused of using member churches' money to supply guns to rebels in Central America.

As I understand its methods, the IRD works with members of conservative groups within mainline churches to gain support for its political programs. Its church-related publication *Faith and Freedom* specifically states that the IRD works "for reform in the Episcopal Church, the United Methodist Church, and the Presbyterian Church (U.S.A.)."[12] Two journals in particular, *Presbyterian Laymen* and *Good News* (Methodist), carry articles consistent with IRD goals, and members of the two are often on the board of the IRD.

In 1993 many women and some men gathered in Minneapolis for the "Re-Imagining Conference," in which members designed liturgies reflecting women's experiences and female images of the sacred and held workshops exploring feminist perspectives on Christian faith. The gathering quickly became controversial. Much of the criticism came from these two journals. *Presbyterian Laymen,* for instance, wrote that conference participants promoted "a new religion with a new god. . . . Rejecting Jesus' divinity and his atonement on the cross, creating a god(dess) in their own image, and affirming lesbian love-making were recurring conference themes."[13] *Good News* noted that the conference was "the most theologically aberrant" the writer had "ever read about."[14]

As a result of such criticism, pressure increased within both denominations, and the possibility of heresy trials was raised. Delores Williams, a presenter at the conference, reported that the Presbyterian church would no longer financially support any of her speaking engagements to Presbyterian events. Black Presbyterians, however, continued to swamp her with invitations.[15]

Following the Re-Imagining Conference, the IRD established an "Ecumenical Coalition on Women and Society." A brochure describing the coalition stated that the first goal was "to study, and, where necessary, counter the detrimental influence of radical feminist ideologies and theologies in our churches and in our society."[16] The brochure defined "radical feminism" as an ideology that sees women as "victims of a patriarchal society . . . manifest[ed] in market economies, western imperialism and orthodox Christian theology."[17]

The IRD also used the Beijing conference, held in September 1995, to promote its challenge to mainline churches. The Beijing conference was one in a series of international women's conferences sponsored by the United Nations. The IRD's quarterly publication *Faith and Freedom* devoted several articles to the conference and to the presence of "goddess worship." It reported, for instance, that "adoration of the goddess was prominent" in the Women's Environment and Development Organization, "funded by the United Methodist Women's Division." And the article concluded by asking, "[Why] this odd turn to paganism?" The article answered, "Idolatry and self-seeking go hand in hand, and the result is social disaster."[18]

THE ROLE OF A PROPHETIC HERITAGE

Although mainline churches have been a significant support and justification for a society and institutions in which some groups have exercised domination over others and the earth, there have always also been voices, within these churches, protesting specific patterns of dominance, oppression, and violence. Certainly, much of the motivation and energy for the continuing stream of liberation movements in the United States and around the world has come from this heritage outside of the mainline churches, but there has been a responsiveness to those movements and even an attempt to learn how to be in solidarity with them. Further, some of the motivation and energy has come from within. There has consistently been an economic critique, for instance, and currently strong challenges from feminists, gays, lesbians, people of color, and those who have been labeled mentally ill and/or disabled.

The result has been increased conflict in many denominations, but this conflict is also a sharpening and clarification about the church's identity and particularly its prophetic heritage. As many commentators have observed, the differences that create profound conflict among mainline churches in the United States today run through, more than between, denominations. Methodist, Presbyterian, Episcopalian, and United Church of Christ members who share a prophetic stance are often much more at home with one another than they are with members of their own denomination who have a significantly different biblical and theological perspective.

I find this situation a blessing. It can be a tremendous opportunity for a church to restructure and for congregations and groups of congregations to emerge with a powerful prophetic commitment. The process will be painful and dislocating, but this history, along with the increasing secularization and the challenge of the Christian Right, can help to open up such churches to the presence of a powerful and transforming spirit of justice and new creation.

U.S. STRUCTURAL ECONOMIC SHIFTS

As the mainline churches are moving toward a crossroads, a major shift in the U.S. economy has been taking place. It is a shift away from the traditional manufacturing base and toward the relocation of manufacturing outside the country and toward an increase in the information and service industries. One need only go shopping to realize the rarity of the "made in the USA" label. Even food is as likely to be imported from outside the country as from other areas of the country. The shopper is least likely to find food grown locally. I still can't get over a fact I learned a couple of years ago: two-thirds of the apples grown in Maine are exported, and Mainers buy apples imported from New York, Washington, and New Zealand!

As this shift occurs, more and more service jobs open up—ranging from a relatively few high-paying legal, medical, and insurance positions, through service technicians, to more modest social service positions, to much-lower-paying tourist-related jobs. This shift, which is already occurring, will mean an increased dichotomy between rich and poor and an ever-larger percentage of the population falling toward poverty.

How this shift will affect white churches remains to be seen. My sense, however, is that many of those who retain high-level economic positions will be inclined to associate with whatever churches remain closest to the political and status center. In turn, this will mean that even fewer financial resources may be available for formerly mainline churches insofar as they continue the movement away from the center.

These changes will be seen as threatening to many. They can, however, be an opportunity for what is left of the mainline church to become a much more prophetic community than it typically has been. Outside forces, in other words, can facilitate a positive transformation of the church toward a community of nurture, celebration, resistance, and witness to new creation. Certainly, as such churches consider their responses to what is happening, there will be conflict and pain. Possibly, however, they will also discern the time as full of grace.

A COMMUNITY JOURNEYING TOWARD TRANSFORMATION

Denominations and congregations will differ in their responses to these developments. The response I trace acknowledges what is happening in this country and the world and seeks a response grounded in a yearning for friendship with God and a renewed and deepened understanding of discipleship to Jesus.[19]

THE COMMUNITY

The following congregation is an imaginary one but typical of many. I will call it Beacon Street United Church of Christ. It is a congregation of 200 members, including me, a membership down from the 350 of fifteen years ago. It has a majority of women and men over sixty years of age and young adults with a scattering of children, with the rest being adults of more or less middle age. Ninety percent are European American; there are a few biracial families—Latino, African American, and European American—and four African American families. The families are largely professional and middle stratra, but about 30 percent are from the working class and a few families are on AFDC and other forms of federal assistance. A couple years ago, we struggled through to a welcoming and affirming stance toward gay and lesbian people in and outside the church, and one new gay couple have become members. Among the elderly members, several have become deaf, and two are in wheelchairs. There are also at least three younger members who have survived stays in psychiatric wards and have been diagnosed by the medical profession as having a bipolar disorder.

Beacon Street is an old church, founded in 1735 on the coast of Maine. It has a modest endowment and a new building that was built when the congregation was much larger than it is now. Its current yearly income is $100,000—from pledges, fund-raisers, fees for the use of the building by community organizations, and endowment interest. With this income, we struggle to meet our financial commitments to a part-time pastor and several part-time positions of music minister, secretary, and youth coordinator, as well as mortgage and building expenses and support of the wider church and participation in local activities.

As congregational members experienced this decline and financial struggle, the initial panic and nostalgia for a time when the church was at the heart of the town's life gradually gave way to a determination not to remain passive and scared. Instead, through small group conversations, Bible study, and worship, we began to draw together and make a radical shift in consciousness. "Our identity and purpose are not tied to size and finances," we said to one another. "We are called to be faithful, not successful by secular standards. What does it mean today to be faithful, to be disciples?" And as that question increasingly came to the forefront of our deliberations, prayers, and study, a new spirit began to be experienced—a spirit of transformation.

A miracle occurred: we began to speak and listen to one another. This was often painful. Some people had to insist on being heard and taken seriously. Many shared experiences of pain and violence that others did not want to believe had happened in this congregation or the wider community. Several made charges of racism and male dominance. People with disabilities spoke of being ignored; old people shared fears and resentments. A few more people left. But those who remained began to hear one another.

In this process, space began to be created for all. It was an uneasy space, full of tension and conflict, pain and guilt. It was also a space for laughter and celebration and embrace. It was a space in which, gradually, all of us had a voice, a space in which even those who said they had nothing to contribute found their voices and shared their experiences and insights. Once we all entered that space, claimed it for our own and voluntarily shared or were forced to share it with others equally, a circle began to replace the old, superficially democratic, hierarchies.

One of the early decisions we made as a result of this miracle was to remove the pews in the sanctuary and replace them with chairs and large pillows, set in concentric circles with an opening, or passage, on the south side of the room, the side closest to the ocean. After extended discussion, we agreed that we saw the ocean as both symbolically and actually the source of life and a powerful metaphor for God. We put the communion table in the middle and the pulpit lectern on the open south side so that all could see whoever was speaking or preaching.

A COMMUNITY OF DISCIPLESHIP

Who is Jesus for us today? Conversation and debate remain lively, heated, and sometimes acrimonious about this question, but there are certain themes we share. One is that whatever theological claims may be made about him, Jesus was a first-century Jew who was nurtured in his religious traditions in a critical and conflict-filled time. An itinerant preacher and healer, he held out a vision of a new society. He proclaimed and taught a pattern of relationships—he called it the kingdom of God—that embraced spiritual, personal, interpersonal, and social dimensions of our lives. As Delores Williams wrote, "The spirit of God in Jesus came to show humans *life*—to show redemption through a perfect *ministerial* vision of righting relations between body (individual and community), mind (of humans and of tradition) and spirit."[20]

Jesus envisioned a society in which the power hierarchies and social barriers of his day would be ended, a society in which the poor and marginalized and despised have food, power, and dignity and are no longer outcast. He envisioned a society of health, a society in which all of us love God from our hearts and love our neighbors as we love ourselves (and we are learning to love ourselves) and in which we live mercifully, gracefully, with one another.

Jesus pointed to this coming reversal in aphorisms, stories, and injunctions. From the records we have, we know that he lived his own life in fidelity to that vision and to the God who will usher in the new age. He ate with the outcasts, he healed, and he remained loyal even when it meant his own death.

We began to understand Jesus' death as a tragic consequence of his life. We saw that his death has meaning in that he refused to change even when it seemed inevitable. We understood that it has meaning also in that, as African Americans and others know too well, people are not necessarily saved from suffering and death at the hands of others. He was a threat to people in power, certainly to the Roman occupation more so than to some Jewish leaders, who did not have that much social power, and he was killed. God did not stop the crucifixion, just as God did not prevent the slave ships from sailing.

Beyond this emerging consensus, we differ deeply about the further significance of Jesus' death and his resurrection. Most believe that Jesus was the "only begotten son of God," and most understand the crucifixion as the significant and redemptive event in Jesus' life. Others see no redemptive meaning in the crucifixion. We also disagree about "what happened" in the resurrection, but we agree that we experience a powerful spirit at work among us, that this is indeed Jesus' spirit and that this spirit speaks to the deepest longings of our hearts for peace, justice, and well-being. We continue to meet Jesus in the wellsprings of our hearts, to be fed by his presence and quickened to live as his disciples. We also affirm that the reality we encounter in Jesus is consistent with the heart of the universe, with God's will for all people. Although not all people may discover that will and well-being through Jesus, for us, Jesus is the Christ.

A COMMUNITY IN ALLIANCE WITH OTHERS

As we engage in exploration and struggle, all our different voices are informing a journey of discovery and reaffirmation. Within the congregation, feminist, womanist, gay and lesbian Christians, and Christians from different social strata and abilities contribute analyses, questions, and theological and ethical directions. Gay and lesbian Christians, Christians of color, working-class and poor Christians, old and young Christians, differently abled Christians, Christians seeking carefully to represent the earth, Christians who have identified more fully with the former status quo—all are a part of the dialogue shaping new theologies, ethics, worship, policy.

But alliance work is not only within the congregation. We have reached out to people in other congregations and outside the church, to individuals and through books. Every member of the congregation participates in some alliance work. One group is learning what it means to be allies with an ecumenical cooperative economic-justice organization in the Dominican Republic. One of the organization's current struggles is finding money for the land it seeks to buy for cooperative farming. We are helping to arrange trips to the town in which the organization is located by North Americans who will come to learn—and pay for—an intensive experience in Spanish language, culture, and justice issues. With these funds, the organization hopes to be able to purchase the needed land.

A large group has been meeting weekly for the past six months to address racism in ourselves, the church, and the local community. The group has joined with African Americans at a nearby air base to work with local school people on more inclusive curricula and on workshops that examine ways in which racism and other forms of oppression shape educational policy and teacher-student relationships and perceptions.

Another group is working with very low income people and economic-justice organizations to collaborate on four fronts: (1) developing a consciousness-raising process for addressing issues of class; (2) trying to ensure that marginalized people are treated with dignity and that necessary assistance is available; (3) envisioning more just economic alternatives; and (4) beginning to develop some examples locally. I will describe this work in more detail toward the end of the chapter.

Still another group meets once a month to sew infant clothes for an ecumenical aid group. The group is mostly older women, but a couple of retired men have joined. Some of the very frail people in the congregation, who may not often come to worship, nevertheless insist on attending these meetings each month. The group provides significant spiritual and emotional support as well as an opportunity to live out their Christian commitment.

A group of people who understand themselves as survivors of the mental health system in the state has organized with allies to address the pervasiveness and insidiousness of stigma and to develop an alternative treatment and healing process.

Another group is working with a local battered women's organization to establish a shelter in the area. Still another group is participating in the activities of the local food bank. Finally, a group is participating with organizations outside the church to address pollution of nearby clam flats. Periodically, representatives from all the other groups meet with this group to explore the ways in which ecological and social issues are intertwined and, in conversations with clammers and others, to determine appropriate actions.

Since not every member participates in each group, we are kept informed through newsletters, through dramatic presentations incorporated into worship services, through books and letters, and through an occasional visit from or to those with whom Beacon Street is in alliance.

BECOMING COMMUNITY

As we study the record about Jesus and listen to God and one another, our community continues to deepen. We are learning—in part because we must in order to survive, in part because our commitment to justice mandates respect and listening as well as speaking—to honor difference and conflict, to express both openly and honestly, and to work through them. As we do this, we grow in our understanding that no one group possesses the truth, that social location and degrees of power and privilege shape our theologies, that God speaks through many messengers, and that we need and are responsible for one another.

One of the ways in which we intentionally nurture community is by organizing ourselves into smaller clusters or extended families that are responsible for the mutual care and support of one another. The clusters are generally three or four households committed to looking out for one another for three years. We have done this by location, grouping together people who live near each other. After the three years, we may decide to do this another way. The clusters ensure that people aren't lonely and isolated and that their physical, emotional, and spiritual well-being is nurtured.

As we take community seriously, we find that we want and need to come together more frequently than we used to. We gather not just to take care of business but also to share our stories, struggles, and activities. We gather to support one another and to be supported. We gather to worship, pray, and study. We are beginning to look like some of the churches of an earlier era, when much of people's lives was centered in the church.

As we continue in this journey of transformation, we are discovering that theology, ethics, and worship matter intensely. New understandings of God emerge as we use inclusive language and images. Images of God's womb, of a disabled God, and of an old or young God startle and dislocate us. A proposal to use names and images of goddesses at first threatened to tear us apart but is now forcing us into profound theological inquiry and reflection. Questions of God's power and the persistence of injustice hound us as we go ever more deeply into the injustice of this country's present and history. Issues of what it means to be created in the image of God leap at us as we struggle to reunite body and spirit and to challenge the Western domination of the natural world. We have found that we need people versed in our heritages, knowledgeable of contemporary developments in feminist, womanist, liberation, and other expressions of theology and ethics, and familiar with worship resources and practices past and present. Such individuals help us to clarify and ground our own reflection, action, and worship so that we can speak and *be* with passion and authority.

Equally, we have discovered that study of issues is important. The commitment to justice and new creation does not mean that a clear choice among limited options exists, and we have learned that it is crucial that we resist the temptation to select short-term and technological solutions to issues of values, power, and institutional pattern, particularly in ecological areas. Modern technology continues to develop and will offer many "answers" to problems of pollution, the use of resources, and waste. "Clean technology" may well become the new buzzword for salvation. But technology, clean or dirty, does not lead to justice even though it may buy us some time. Only a commitment to do justice leads to justice.

Further, and surprisingly, this journey has also led to a renascence of creative expression of our faith(s). Drama, music, visual and verbal art forms, and dance are beginning to flower. The sanctuary, narthex, and fellowship hall have become performance and exhibit spaces. On occasion, this creativity informs worship, but often it is in addition to worship and becomes an opportunity for us to share our vocation and insights with the wider community.

To equip us with the resources and leadership necessary for these activities, we are considering that we should modify the minister's job description to include more time for theological reading, reflection, and writing and research into worship resources and possibilities. Other congregational members are volunteering to make similar changes and take on more extended and specific responsibilities for the community and its life. As a congregation, we are learning to take seriously the old Protestant principle of the priesthood of all believers.

The emphasis on our identity as disciples, the importance of community, the commitment to justice in alliance, and the discovery of the role and excitement of study have led us to experiment with new patterns of leadership and decision-making. As the congregation becomes more aware of how our beliefs and values are shaped by our ecosocial locations, we seek volunteers from each location reflected in the congregation to serve as a coordinating council, along with representatives from the many worship and action groups in the congregation. This council meets periodically to share information and attend to issues that arise, and it tries to ensure that all members still know that they have a voice in the congregation and are valued members. If there is a problem, the council or an individual member calls for a special hearing, a time to speak or mediate or in some other appropriate way address and resolve the situation. At least twice a year, the congregation meets as a whole to review where we are, evaluate our witness, and envision, dream, or plan some aspect of the future.

SPIRITUAL LIFE AND WORSHIP

Beacon Street Church has become, by choice and by necessity, increasingly open to God. We do not worship God because we believe that God should or wants to be praised. Even though Jesus speaks of the kingdom of God, he does not reveal a God who is a feudal sovereign but one who cares for the sparrow and the person with leprosy—in his image, a father.

We worship because we need to and long to. In worship, we set aside a time to open ourselves to the presence of God. We confess the concrete ways we have denied our discipleship and seek restoration of broken relationships. Perhaps, above all, worship offers us—rather stiff, white middle-class Protestants—an opportunity to express our love of and delight in God, to experience communion and even, if we dare, ecstasy.

We have become very intentional about the ways that worship can facilitate our many responses to God. Worship occurs several times a week and takes many forms. It no longer occurs only or even primarily on Sunday morning. In fact, because of people's work schedules and other responsibilities, a Monday-evening worship preceded by a potluck supper has replaced Sunday morning as the major occasion. But there is also worship on several mornings, afternoons, and evenings each week. On Tuesday at 6:30 A.M. a group gathers for a guided meditation, singing, and breakfast. On Thursday evening, a service conducted in Central American Spanish is attended by people from other churches and the wider community. A service at Wednesday noon offers a Bible study and prayers. On Friday morning, a group of feminist women gather to experiment with original liturgies, share their stories, and explore theological themes. And on Friday evening, people gather for a communion service.

Whole-congregation worship uses patterns that most powerfully enable all of us to hear and respond to God and one another. Therefore, its components are agreed on. New dimensions are introduced only after discussion and general acceptance. At the same time, every effort is made to honor the diversity of the congregation, including age and cultural background. Readings and hymns may include more than one language, with translations available orally or in writing. Two members have learned signing, and this has become a standard feature. We have discovered that in its almost dancelike movement, signing adds a richness to the worship for all.

The content of worship also varies from week to week. At least once a month, we spend a large block of time in silent meditation or prayer. Typically, there is a sermon, but we may discuss a text or theme instead. Occasionally, someone leads us in a guided meditation. Again, the variations grow out of congregation decision, need, and time of year.

As we addressed the need for appropriate language and images in worship, we made a number of significant decisions. Although inclusive language is taken for granted, at the same time we are careful not to mask significant differences among women and men of different social groups. Images and language that include non-human reality are also, of course, an intrinsic part of worship.

Further, we take care that inclusive language does not rewrite the past in such a way as to deny either the oppressiveness of the past or its spiritual power and legacy. For instance, we decided to repeat occasionally the "Gloria Patri" as a historical statement, fully recognizing that its sexist language has helped perpetuate an oppressive theology. No part of our past is necessarily or automatically normative for today until the congregation consciously affirms its authority. When the language of the past is simply made inclusive and incorporated into worship, it obscures the reality we must affirm: its normativeness is problematic until a congregation decides, as a result of theological wrestling, to affirm it as normative. Addressing issues of language is only half the task.

Our worship draws on ancient and modern written, musical, visual, and dramatic materials. We also create our own materials. Children contribute plays, prayers, and stories. One member has written a hymn. Another taught the congregation some of songs she sings in a women's spirituality group. Still another member brought to worship a one-sentence affirmation that he asked the congregation to chant with him.

The celebration of the sacraments of communion and baptism is central to our congregational life, although we have changed them significantly. Communion has become less a remembering of Jesus' death for us and more a remembering of Jesus' life and the peasants with whom he associated—the people whose food may have been largely some bread and wine—a remembering that Jesus' life with them led to his death. It is a reminder that our standing in that tradition as disciples can lead to becoming failures in the world's eyes and can even lead, on occasion, to our deaths. And yet, at the same time, such is the richness of the activity and its symbolism that we also remember Jesus' resurrection: around the table we are equal, we each take a comparable amount of bread and wine. As an acquaintance of mine has said, communion is the only ritual act of the church in which we all already share equally in God's new creation. It is indeed a foretaste of the coming realm of God.

We have attempted to restore the religious significance of infant baptism, to redeem it from its cultural significance. It is a major occasion and an extended celebration. When a baby or other individual is baptized, several members take turns holding or standing with the one to be baptized, and there is a searching discussion, not just a recited formula, of the meaning of incorporating this person into this community and the body of Christ. Parents or the individuals themselves help plan the service, choosing music and other elements that have special meaning to them. The congregation in turn chooses music or other elements that it especially wishes to share with those entering into the life of the church.

A covenant of membership is another major occasion and celebration in the life of the congregation. Often the entire service is designed around making such a commitment. It is indeed like a marriage and demands preparation, commitment, and learning to live together. A group in the congregation is charged with all three. In the preparation, they share with the member-to-be who and what the congregation is—its heritage, vision for the future, strengths and weaknesses, needs, responsibilities, and vocation. In turn, the prospective member shares her/his journey, hopes, and fears. During this time, the group and the member-to-be explore the individual's ecosocial location as well as those of other congregational members, the congregation's commitment to the work of justice, and some of the implications of this for the person's life. The congregation, through the small group, and the prospective member also explore what each has to contribute to enrich the life of both.

The new member is then asked to support the congregation with finances as she or he is able, as well as with work, with prayer, and with participation in the congregation's mission and justice work. These commitments are to be quite concrete (e.g., "I will work with the anti-racism task force for the next year"). Then the group and the prospective member design the service, combining elements that have by now become traditional parts of a covenant ceremony and elements that have been selected especially for this occasion. Included in the service is a time for the new member and the congregation to covenant with one another, for the new person to share her/his pledges, and for the congregation to share theirs. Finally, the new member will become part of a neighborhood group.

We renew our commitments to God and one another every two years, as part of the annual meeting. This is preceded by a period of reflection, prayer, study, meditation, and analysis about the congregation, the local community, the wider church, and the world. We ask ourselves questions about our individual and corporate fidelity to Jesus' vocation, the extent to which our life together nurtures and challenges us, what specific responsibilities we should undertake, what alliances we should build, which responsibilities we should discontinue, and what resources we need to fulfill our commitments. Then, as with new members, we covenant together very concretely, making pledges in all areas of the congregation's life—justice action, alliance-building, nurture and support, worship, finances, outreach.

On occasion, we celebrate commitments among individuals. A moving covenant was recently celebrated among four elderly women, all of whom were widows and had become inseparable friends. They wrote and celebrated a ceremony of friendship that included commitments to share financial resources as much as they possibly could, to care for one another if one became ill or needed nursing care, and in principle to do everything possible to enable each one to avoid having to go to a nursing home. We also celebrate covenants made between couples, regardless of sexual orientation.

We believe that it is very important that covenants made between individuals include friends and families and if possible a spiritual community that also pledges support and advocacy for the couple. When such a covenant is between members of the congregation, therefore, all the members are urged to participate and to make specific commitments. Again, these are discussed ahead of time and are incorporated into the ceremony.

In addition to the above, we have developed other ceremonies for special occasions. We have elder rituals for women and men who have reached the age of sixty-five. We celebrate the time of menarche for young women and the entrance of boys into young manhood. And we have developed ceremonies of ending and new beginning for relationships that have changed from the original commitments.

We also celebrate the seasons in addition to the church year. Solstice and equinox have become major ceremonies for the congregation. These ceremonies help draw us closer to the natural world and to the rhythms of death and birth—planting, germinating, harvesting. As we celebrate, however, we also recognize that impoverishment, pain, and pollution have been and often still are part of these activities. The rituals combine, therefore, spiritual, political, and physical dimensions of our lives with God.

Finally, a healing circle is available to anyone who requests it. This is usually a simple laying on of hands, accompanied by chanting, singing, or silent or verbal prayer. Often the person wishing a healing rite shares her/his journey into pain, grief, illness, crisis, injury, or violation before the rite and discusses how the community can be of support in the continuing journey. We recognize that God's healing power circulates among us and that a person who is in pain or is suffering often especially needs to be embraced and affirmed as a central part of the community.

WITNESS

It is critically important to resist oppression and seek a measure of justice through traditional public means: to lobby and testify for legislative changes; to demonstrate and boycott against unjust practices and organizations. Such actions need to be conducted locally and nationally, as well as at the state house. We participate in these actions in the contexts of our alliance work. We may also participate in response to urgent action appeals from the national church and other justice advocates. It is also critical that we incarnate personally our vision of justice and new creation and develop alternative practices that might also lead to more just structures.

At Beacon Street Church, our alliance work and study have led us increasingly to focus on the role of economic patterns and the ways they connect with other forms of oppression. Specifically, we have been exploring practices that nurture sustainable livelihood and ecosocial justice and how these might relate to each other very practically and concretely where Beacon Street Church is located.

For instance, while we have been working with the state legislature in an attempt to restore some of the cuts legislated by the 1996 federal "welfare reform" legislation, we have also agreed that we should develop a structure that offers everyone equal access to food, clothing, and shelter. We can't do this on a national level, but we can begin on the local level. So we have taken the following steps. We have agreed that everyone in the congregation can learn to compost and that those who are knowledgeable will help start compost piles for each household. We have also planted a common garden in a church-owned area behind the church. Some of the compost is taken to this site. Crews sign up for a week at a time—with leaders who are knowledgeable about organic gardening—to prepare, cultivate, and harvest vegetables and herbs. We hold a weekly "freeze-in" in the church kitchen to freeze, dry, and can the food for all the congregation's households. Since many members have gardens of their own, their excess is added to the food from the freeze-ins. A few members hunt, and they provide a supply of meat for those who want it.

Before we embarked on this project, we sat down with a local organization of women on AFDC, with the staff of a battered women's shelter, and with some residents from the growing local Cambodian community. Together, we designed the project and determined the guidelines for participation. We held a mammoth bean supper to raise money for the initial investment in plowing, tools, seed, seedlings, and other materials.

It has taken a couple of years for the land to bear abundantly, but this past summer produced a bumper crop that has filled our larders for the winter. Since this harvest means that we will have to buy few vegetables, those who can are setting aside some of the money saved, to purchase seeds and other supplies as well as to establish a fund for those years when the garden may produce only a little. Also, some of us are beginning to explore the possibility of building a greenhouse, which will extend the Maine growing season.

And we are broadening such nonmonetary economic activity into a community bartering system. With two hundred members, the congregation has tremendous resources and skills. Carpentry, plumbing, teaching, sewing, cooking, child care, legal services, gardening, massage, financial knowledge, computer use, access to the

Internet, dental care, window washing, transportation, cutting wood, mowing lawns, storytelling, creating art—the list is practically endless. Such a system will involve children as well as adults, old people as well as young. Everyone has something to offer, everyone can receive. When there is no fee and fee differentials, everyone can contribute and receive equally.

One of the areas we think we can include in this system, at least to some extent, is health and medical care, particularly dental care. Some folks can offer workshops on prevention and on wellness. And we are talking with those who have the requisite skills and knowledge about being available to anyone who is part of the bartering community for checkups, therapeutic massage, some medical treatment, acupuncture, homeopathic remedies, and other services.

One of our unanswered questions at this date is whether we should form such a bartering community within the congregation or whether we should, as we did with the gardening, extend the circle into the local community. We will probably choose the latter.

Since we do live in a monetary economy, we have also begun to create ways to provide some income for people. For instance, one of the women on AFDC has been studying to be a mechanic. Some members of the congregation have been providing some financial assistance for her; in return, she is maintaining and/or repairing their cars in a garage space and with tools made available by another congregational member.

One of the most exciting activities we have become a part of is working with a group of low-income women who have formed a community land trust. The local community-action agency receives housing subsidies, through grants, to help purchase homes. In the $40,000-to-$60,000 range, these houses are generally in need of repair or renovation. The family who will own the house must get a mortgage from a local bank for the difference between the subsidy and the cost of the house, typically a mortgage that is between $200 and $300 a month. If that family moves and decides to sell the house, the family will receive the equity they put into it, but the subsidy stays with the house, making it affordable for the next buyer. Members of the community land trust, families, and church members work together on the repair and renovation. Some materials are donated by interested businesses, and as with the garden, everyone joins in preparing a New England bean supper to raise other money. Tourists love these suppers: they get an abundant meal of three kinds of baked beans, ham, brown bread, innumerable casseroles, salads, and homemade pies, and they contribute to a worthwhile enterprise at the same time!

A small group in the congregation is beginning to address issues of tax justice. And a few members are challenging the rest of us to go a step further, closer to the early church. They are urging us to determine what kind of income—top as well as bottom—is just and donate any above the top level to a pool; a certain percentage of this donation would be available to anyone in the church, and the rest would be invested, with the income to be used for justice work in the wider society. We are still struggling with this idea. Much study and further consciousness-raising is needed.[21]

In all of the congregation's activities, we have found that sustained action is absolutely essential. Too much of what has been called "social action" has been intermittent, atomistic, faceless, and voiceless. A letter to a legislator, a check in the offering plate, a discussion of poverty, a demonstration, even a boycott—all are essential actions, but they keep us at a distance from others, and from ourselves. Only as we become part of the ongoing struggle for justice, sustainability, and well-being in concert with others, particularly with others who are different from ourselves, will our hearts continue to open. God speaks to us concretely through the voices of all her people, plants, and animals. Women and men of all social locations in and out of the church must insist on speaking and being heard. Others must come to our support and help create the space for speaking and hearing. At the same time, we must put ourselves into positions to hear and respond to other voices. As white feminist Christians, we can work together, support one another, build alliances with other women anywhere, and come together also with men who are willing to learn and/or are committed to an inclusive justice. It's a long journey, but we are not alone. If we are faithful, slowly—and sometimes quickly—the dividing walls of hostility are broken; new insights, wisdom, and energies are gained; power is shared, and reconciliation is possible. Then we can move into God's future, a future shaped by the hope of new creation.

"You shall love the Sovereign your God with all your heart, and with all your soul, and with all your strength, and with all your mind; and your neighbor as yourself." the Sovereign your God with all your heart, and with all your strength, and with all your mind; and your neighbor as yourself."

2

METHODS OF CONVERSATION

AND COMMITMENT

The master's tools will never dismantle the master's house.
—*Audre Lorde*, Sister Outsider

What happens in white feminism if we begin to give up *all* the master's tools and not just some?
—*Susan Thistlethwaite*, Sex, Race, and God

In this chapter, I seek to develop a theological method consistent with my feminist commitments and the life of the congregation described in the preceding chapter. It is a method that acknowledges who we are in this congregation, these ecosocial locations—working in alliance, worshiping God, and seeking to remain open to individual and corporate transformation in the church and world. It is, thus, a method that acknowledges the particularities of our experience and yet dares to speak of a God who transcends those particularities.

I understand this method as an ongoing conversation with other feminists and womanists, with my own spiritual, political, and personal experiences, and with an expanding circle of voices, including the natural world. Not all voices are equal, and their ecosocial location must always be recognized. To that conversation I bring my own commitments; as a result of the conversation, I revise and strengthen my commitments. In what follows, I will explore selected methodological issues that are central to my own unfolding commitments.

CONTEXT AND CONDITION

Recognizing ecosocial location, I describe my methodological starting point and standing place in the phrase "context and condition." The word "context" refers to location—who I am and where I stand as a white feminist woman doing theology. It acknowledges the integrity of my voice and also its relativity. "Condition" refers to the fact that all theology is so located, that there is no universal or transcendent place to stand. All theology is contextual; that is the condition of theology.

This does not mean that theology is only relative; it means that theology is concretely relational. If we, as white feminists, are not to repeat the false universalizing of the dominant theological traditions, we must become more aware of the actual relationships that shape our theologizing and make some choices about which relationships should shape it. Delores Williams has written: "The choice of language and issues suggests with whom a group or community wants to be in relation and dialogue. Current feminist fascination with theory and epistemology indicates the serious degree to which white feminists want to be in relation and dialogue with white males. . . . Further, I think it indicates that many white feminists do not really want to destroy the master's house . . . because this house provides the sustenance for their psychic and material survival."[1] She states her challenge: "The question is Do we feminist-womanist women dare trust each other enough to transcend the awful brutal history of white-women-black-women relations and come together to create a free future for *all* women?"[2]

That is obviously a critical question and challenge. For me, the answer is *yes!* Doing theology is as much an activity of listening to the voices of others as it is sharing my own voice; it is a respectful dialogue, not a monologue. Theology should be a reciprocal process, a conversation of courage, vulnerability, and accountability.

The relationality of theology means that I am in conversation first of all with other feminists and womanists, and I hold myself accountable to them. These include women both in and outside of academia. They include women I have been working in alliance with. They cut across all the social barriers of race, class, sexuality, abilities, and age. They are the women I read and talk with, professionally and personally. They form the immediate circle in which I stand.

But there are also wider circles—of other people and of nonhuman species. I am accountable to them in that I must listen to and for their voices, particularly to those who have had no voice. I have a responsibility not to stereotype or discount their experiences and struggles, and although I initially interpret them in the feminist framework I have been given, that framework is eventually modified by their voices.

Listening to the voices of nonhuman species is extremely difficult, and there is great danger of anthropomorphizing those voices. But we must make the effort, drawing on the many resources we have—human voices articulating a diversity of experiences with plant and animal species, direct mystical experiences, and the understandings and experiences of those who bring other cultural frameworks to their relationships with the natural world. Out of all of these, we can begin to articulate a nonoppressive understanding of our similarities to and differences from the rest of creation.

Ultimately these circles of human and nonhuman voices are embraced in a wider circle I call God. Ultimately I am accountable to God for what I do and say, but this relationship also is an ongoing conversation that is informed by voices in the other circles.

As I affirm the above contexts and conditions, I have also come to affirm another one—the church, specifically the United Church of Christ. I have chosen to affirm my Christian legacy, with all its problems and oppressiveness as well as its resources. The church nurtured my experience of the love of God and my commitment to justice, which I understand as a central part of the practical love of myself and my neighbor. And as I said in the introduction, for all their faults, Christian and Jewish religious institutions do have a commitment to justice as central to their missions.

I do, however, stand on the margins of the traditional church—I am not yet in the Beacon Street congregation. To borrow a phrase from bell hooks, I seek, with others, to make the margins a place of creativity, power, and transformation. I seek, in concert with others, to take the initiative in constructing our own theologies without apology, theologies for a world in which the church no longer primarily supports the status quo but is a community of survival, protest, hope, and even transformation. The resources—past, present, and future—for developing such a church, a post-Christendom church, are not simply given to us; to some extent we have to create them, along with the theologies, but that enterprise will be an exciting task!

Context and condition, therefore, point to a theological method that is relative and relational. It is a conversation among many voices, including my own—voices not yet all equal.

WOMEN'S (AND MEN'S) EXPERIENCE

Women's experience, as a source for feminist theology, includes the wide diversity of women in different ecosocial locations. It also includes the daily experience of being women in this culture, specific spiritual experience, and the struggle for justice. For instance, for many women, daily life is a struggle simply to survive physically. Most women—all women?—struggle to survive psychically, although some may have buried this struggle so deeply that they are unaware of it. Some of the daily experiences not only are different but also are shaped by women's diverse classes, races, ages, abilities, and sexual locations.

Some women have been characterized and treated as animals, beasts of burden, fit only to do menial work and to care for another's children. Other women have been petted and protected, given messages that they are goddesses or fragile pieces of bone china. Both groups have been denied their humanity, but in radically different ways and with radically different consequences to themselves, to their relations with one another, to their way of being in the world, and to their experience of God.

Some women have worked with land that someone else owns and have experienced physical agony from their labor and the grinding down of their spirit. Others have worked land that they own and have seen it fail them. Still others have experienced the earth (even the name changes) primarily as escape and renewal from the burdens and responsibilities of daily life. Such diversity is then brought into theological reflection.

Feminist and womanist social analyses criticize the distribution of power that enables a few to have access to a highly disproportionate amount of the resources and privileges of a society or of the world. Social patterns that entitle white heterosexual men in the United States to take from the rest of the world, to use the rest of the world for the welfare of a few, and to govern what the rest of the world receives in return are simply wrong.

These social analyses also uncover and judge the many forms of violence that are threatened and/or used to maintain these patterns. Malnutrition, battering, low self-esteem, war, denying people a voice, and control of cultural institutions are all forms of violence that keep subjected groups subject. These social analyses also critique and judge the cultural and religious beliefs and values that support and sanction the patterns. Racism, patriarchy, classism, heterosexism, ableism, ageism, and humanism (humans over the earth) are wrong. They are unjust. They are contrary to God's will for God's creation.

The linchpin in these patterns is power, and feminist and womanist social analyses challenge a hierarchical distribution of power. The same critique must then be made of theological understandings of power. Any construction of God that attributes to God significantly disproportionate power is suspect. The constructions were made during the times of monarchies and empires, when the Christian God was imaged as king and Jesus as proclaiming and ushering in God's kingdom. Although the political patterns have changed somewhat, entrenched hierarchies still remain and with them the implicit theological justification in the way we continue to talk about God.

Finally, a similar diversity exists regarding direct spiritual experience. My reading of womanists suggests that the experience of God is not of a God who imposes further limits or constraints, who is over against, but who is *with* them in the struggle. Much of life is a struggle for survival, but power for that struggle is deepened and sustained by God's presence. My reading of white feminists and my own experience point to a somewhat different experience of God. God is one in whom we delight, from whom we receive delight, with whom we are bound in mutual embrace. Our relationship with God is an experience of mutuality or friendship, and it is not accidental that friendship has been a theme in white feminist writing much more than it has been in womanist writing.

This wealth of women's experience should inform feminist theology in at least two ways. It contributes to the content of theology, and it cautions the theologian against universalizing. I have a responsibility to take my experience seriously, to use it. At the same time, as I consider its significance, I must examine my experience in relation to the experiences of other women. In short, I cannot do feminist theology that is not grounded in alliance.

Above, I included men's experience parenthetically as a source for feminist theology. If we draw only on women's experience—and relate our theologies back only to women—we will eventually repeat some of the errors of traditional theology. Men's experience—I am thinking primarily of white men at this point—is part of human experience, after all. The task is to examine men's experience in light of their struggle for justice, in light of the kinds of analyses and alliance work that many women have been doing. I invite white male theologians, ethicists, activists, and worshipers to begin their work with the statement, "I am a white [whatever class, abilities, age, and geographical and sexual locations] man; my understanding of God, the world, and my role in it has been shaped by these locations in the following ways . . ." *Then* men can begin to determine what is of value in their heritages and what they have to contribute to ongoing theological conversations.

THE BIBLE AND JESUS

The Bible was not written for us. It was written in a different historical period, to and for people of different historical cultures, all of which were quite different in many ways from our own. It contains assumptions and injunctions that many of us simply reject. It is no longer the "word of God" in any obvious or unqualified sense.

Understanding the thoroughly historical and often problematic context and content of the biblical material puts significant constraints on how I think of the Bible as a resource, and especially as an authority for theology, ethics, and the life of the church. I can't proof text; I can't isolate certain passages and make those normative at the expense of others, although there are certainly sections I agree with more than others. I can't lift out certain sections, for example, the prophets, and find in them a "usable past," to use Letty Russell's phrase. The same prophets who charged their people with denying their responsibility to poor people also inveighed against them for worshiping some of the goddesses I honor. Some of their pictures of women are negative, and the prophets image God in ways I reject. I have a similar difficulty with wisdom images and passages and the effort in current feminist literature to connect Christ with the feminine persona of Sophia, ignoring the contexts and indeed the bulk of the wisdom literature. Similarly, the Gospel accounts are culturally located (they couldn't be anything else). They reflect the concerns, language, images, and issues of people in cultures and social structures in many ways significantly different from our own.

More important, we are separated from the story of Jesus not only by history but also by nearly two thousand years of privileged Western interpretation. Our task may not be so much to get behind the Gospel accounts to the historical Jesus, although I do find that search interesting and helpful, as to allow our minds and hearts to be converted to hear the story of a man whose life challenges most of what we white people take for granted. As Luise Shottroff wrote in her study of women's everyday life in Jesus' time, the New Testament was "better understood by the peasants of Solentiname than by the women and men in the first world's biblical scholarship; the peasants of Solentiname lived in a political and economic situation comparable to that of the Jesus movement."[3] I would add other groups, including African Americans and those in similar political and economic situations in this country. Those of us who have traditionally had some connection with the dominant society have to work our way through centuries in which the gospel was spiritualized and individualized if we are to begin to hear the story central to, but buried deep within, our heritage. How then might we think about the Bible?

I begin by recognizing that my interpretation of a biblical text is my responsibility; it is my act. I can no longer claim that it is *the normative* understanding. Just as we have to take responsibility for our theology, so we must take responsibility for our use of the Bible. Second, I *must* read, write, and meditate in the context and condition of one committed to ending injustice and working for a more fulfilling life for all creatures. I must work in the context of liberation, with feminist-womanist and biblical scholars and activists who continue to nurture me. Third, I then bring my own heart to the reading and interpretation, seeking to become a participant in a conversation that transcends two thousand years.

As I meditate on and study the stories about Jesus, I see, as do many others today, a man who was a leader in one of the many Jewish liberation movements of that era. He stood with the marginalized, the outcast. Specifically, he stood with the landless poor as well as those stigmatized by illness or by political or ethnic identity. He denied that such ostracism was God's will. He described a God who challenges wealth, social authority, and privilege, who has special concern for the "least," seeks their inclusion into the community, ends their pain, frees them from debt, and feeds them, and who liberates prisoners—presumably political prisoners—and demolishes walls between ethnic, political, and social groups, between Jews, Romans, and Samaritans, between men and women.

This construction of Jesus compels my love and commitment. It speaks to my heart, and I dare to affirm that it is consistent with the heart of the universe. And perhaps what is most important for me is that I understand Jesus' life as reflecting a power at work in the universe to challenge and overcome injustice and brokenness.

If we are not part of that vocation, we should be. If we are, we are not alone in our struggle for justice, our outrage at violence, our grief at wasted and destroyed lives. There is a spirit-power supporting, inspiring, challenging, and meeting us—taking up residence, so to speak, in the deepest part of our own hearts.

At the same time, I am aware that this understanding of Jesus is a construction. I have learned about it not only from reading the Bible but also from reading liberation theologies, participating in justice work, worshiping, and addressing my own racism and other forms of unearned social advantages.

Given all the above, I have found that the Bible is not authoritative but *contributes to* an authoritative voice. For all the transcendent appeal and challenge of Jesus' teaching and life, they are nevertheless related to the contexts and conditions of his time. I listen to Jesus with utter seriousness, but at the same time I try to open myself to God as God is at work in the contexts and conditions of our time, including our diverse experiences as women. (The fact that most of us who are white have not faced a cross may well indicate that we have yet to take those themes seriously enough.) My task is to continue the work of the church, to be part of the circle of listening to God, by understanding what is happening today—including how our interpretation of God is shaped by images and concepts of our time—and by attending to scriptural voices for insights and challenges.

To affirm that the Bible contributes to an authoritative voice sets us free from having to manipulate it. Jesus' teaching about love, for instance, is a part of our heritage that we can bring to a discussion about economic justice; but this is just one consideration among others. We take his teaching seriously, but we have to determine whether and/or how it relates to the concern under consideration. The New Testament records many stories of Jesus' healing people, stories that had both political and spiritual meaning to his hearers but that are not necessarily normative for us. Our understanding of illness is significantly different, and we have assumptions and stigmas that we must address. As feminists, we should develop theologies of wholeness and healing, but they are our theologies, developed out of the circle described above. Too often the effort to make the healing miracles normative for ill people today has resulted in cruelty toward people who have been labeled "disabled" or "ill." The Bible thus contributes to—it does not contain—a normative picture of Jesus, theology, and ethics.

ETHICS

For me, a post-Christendom Christian feminist theology supports people's and the earth's struggles to survive and to move toward ecological (social, spiritual, and biological) and personal transformations of justice, healing, and well-being. This is the theology's shape, its beginning and end. It is grounded in traditional biblical themes of new creation, the kingdom of God, a messianic banquet, a new heaven and earth.

It is also grounded in people's and the earth's struggle to survive, a struggle at odds with traditional theological emphases on sacrifice, whether this be the sacrifice of Christ or our imitative sacrifice out of love for our neighbor.

The feminist theology I am constructing is thus an ethical theology. It is also an ecological theology. It is shaped by specific ethical principles—inspired by my understanding of Jesus' vision but delineated in light of our twentieth-century feminist-womanist insights and experiences. The principles of particular importance to me are justice, sustainability, and well-being.

Justice is foundational. A theology that reflects and/or justifies unjust relationships, whether institutional, interpersonal, or cosmic, is a theology of injustice and not worth my time or energy, much less the commitment to the power(s) of the universe about whom theology seeks to speak.

What, then, is justice? Justice moves a society toward equal distribution of power, equal access to resources, and social respect for the diversity of human and nonhuman life. Justice is thus political, economic, cultural, and spiritual.

At its heart, justice is equally shared social power, power ultimately shared cosmically. This has profound implications for how we think about God as well as about human relationships and human–natural world relationships, implications I will explore in the section on theology.

There are many kinds of power, some of which are more closely connected to justice than others. Personal power, for instance, is that capacity within a person—and, for all we know, within many other forms of life—to survive, to fight to live. It exists in unjust conditions as well as just. It is the power of the slave to resist, perhaps the power of the plant to come up through the cement. A just society nurtures that kind of power but does not create it.

There is another form of personal power, often called "charisma." This is the power to move others, sometimes against tremendous obstacles. Again, a just society does not create that power but will respect it.

The kind of power that is most directly associated with justice is institutional, or social, power—the power available to some groups and individuals by virtue of where they are in a society. Typically that power is distributed in a hierarchical fashion, with decision-making capacity, responsibility, and authority concentrated in the upper levels. Such a structure is unjust and should be equalized.

Shared social power is essential for at least two compelling reasons. One is that hierarchical power breeds and reflects oppression. There must be some kind of justification for those in power to be in power, and that justification, at least in Western culture, has been consistently accompanied by a racist, patriarchal, religious, or some other (including species) claim that assigns more value, more *humanity* to the groups on top. Further, structures of dependency, control of access to resources, and violence are set up to maintain the status quo.

Connected to this reason is my understanding that reality is inherently full of conflict. Different groups and different individuals have different insights, interests, values, and needs. These cannot all be represented by a few in power. Benevolent dictatorships are still dictatorships.

But there is also a second reason that shared social power is essential. Shared social power is more consistent with personal power than with hierarchical forms of power. The power of our internal life can and should be expressed, in consort with others, in all areas of life. I don't know if that is a universal claim that can be made about creaturely life, but I suspect it is, and for me it is part of a desirable social construction of human and nonhuman nature.

More equally shared power should be the norm. Within such a society, however, various temporary inequalities can and probably should exist. These can range from power differentials between babies and adults, for instance, to leadership positions. Individuals and groups can be given a preponderant degree of power and/or responsibility for specific periods of time. Representative forms of power can also be developed, again for specific periods of time and/or responsibilities. But the context and expectations are shared power, within which temporary unequal power resides. Today, for most of us, it is the other way around.

Access to resources by all creatures, not only human beings, is the second dimension of justice. Further, there should be *sufficient* resources, not simply to survive or meet basic needs but to live with dignity, grace, and well-being, to develop one's interests and talents, to live deeply.

There are many unresolved issues in the idea of sufficient access to resources. For example, what is sufficient and how is this determined? To what extent are the resources produced locally, regionally, globally? If sufficiency allows for some disparity, how is that determined? These are all issues that will be explored later. My purpose here is simply to be clear about the normative principles that shape the theology I am developing.

Finally, justice includes social and institutional respect for biological, cultural, and historical diversity. It respects differences without arranging them on a hierarchical scale of better or worse, more or less. A just society is one in which racial differences, for instance, are celebrated, in which the historical tragedies around those differences are remembered and understood and new ways of constructing race are created. Similarly, a just society is one in which poison ivy is respected and valued for itself as well as for any use it may have for others and is not simply devalued because it can poison.

Sustainability is also an essential norm. I believe that a criterion of an adequate or true theology must reflect a commitment to shape action toward a sustainable universe. Without sustainability, nothing else is possible. To disregard it is a denial of justice, a continuation of the condemned violence and genocide perpetrated on human beings.

Actually, in sustainability I include both the human and the nonhuman. I include ecosystems with the diversity of humanity in them. They should continue. But sustainability does not mean the absence of change in ecosystems; however, changes that bring death should be gradual and "in the fullness of time," not abrupt and cataclysmic, insofar as we have a role in making those changes. Changes should be such that relatively small adaptations can enable us to continue to live; or changes should be repairable. They should not be such that an ecosystem and its inhabitants cannot renew themselves or cannot evolve into a new and sustainable ecosystem.

Well-being is the final principle I wish to mention. Well-being is an enhanced quality of life. It is not to be confused with normalcy or with stereotypical understandings of health or wholeness or with a certain IQ level. Rather, it is living well, enjoying life, living in the midst of beauty as well as pain. It is having the opportunity to develop one's interests and talents as fully as one can. It is living a life of mutuality and spiritual depth: enjoying relationships of love, affection, friendship, and care; knowing that one is loved and cared for by others and the universe; being able to enjoy the body-spirit of oneself and others—human and nonhuman. It is living a life of personal meaning in communities of shared meaning. It is valuing one's heritage and contributing to the common good.

THE ROLE OF DIFFERENT TRADITIONS IN THEOLOGICAL CONSTRUCTION

How should white feminists regard non-Christian traditions, Judaism, and non-white Christian traditions as we develop a feminist theology? I have in mind specifically North American indigenous traditions, Christian traditions that have been marginalized by dominant Christian cultures and institutions, Judaism, and European goddess traditions. All of these traditions include feminists, womanists, *mujeristas,* and others who are committed to justice and who are doing valuable, exciting, creative, and appealing work in understanding, analyzing, and reconstructing theologies, liturgies, rituals, spiritualities, and ethics. The temptation for white feminists has been to take anything that helps—from wherever we can get it.

We are, however, gradually becoming more aware that this is part of the exploitation and continuing oppression of other traditions. To criticize or to appropriate any of these traditions is to continue the stance of the conqueror. However well-intentioned we may be or however hungry for meaningful spirituality we may be, our ecosocial location is one of social power and unearned privilege. We are simply once again taking what we want.

Further, in so doing, we falsify the tradition we are appropriating. When we turn to another culture's religion, we abstract it from its history and social context and ignore the complex relationship that exists among spirituality, theology, and society, a relationship that gives the religion its own integrity and its own ways of affirming and/or challenging a given status quo. In abstracting it, appropriation falsifies the religion.

Such appropriation can minimize our responsibility for social consequences. The appropriated religion becomes an individual or communal spiritual practice divorced from a responsible relation to a history. If a non-Indian is going to adopt an indigenous spiritual practice, she or he should become Indian, that is, become immersed in a historical community with other Indians who are rooted in that same history. Right now, that is not likely to occur except in exceptional circumstances.

The question of African American and other Christian traditions, as well as our relationship to Judaism, is different from but also similar to that of indigenous traditions. White Christians share many traditions with Christians of color and with Jews. At the same time, there are basic differences, some of which are further complicated by class differences within each group. But here, as with indigenous traditions, the relationship is one of power differential. Appropriation becomes exploitation and falsification. I am deeply uneasy, for instance, when I sing spirituals. They have come out of such pain and courage that I feel as if I am trivializing them by singing them as a part of a worship service. Writing from the marginalized side, Judith Plaskow makes this point also: "Every time I see the word *shalom* in Christian feminist work, . . . I feel a knot in my stomach. . . . I think there is something about the use of the Hebrew word that implies kinship, familiarity, and sense of ease with Judaism, a feeling of 'we're all in this together,' that's false or premature."[4]

We do this in so many ways. I remember when Katie Cannon told me of a white colleague who wanted to drop the term "feminist" when she discovered the term "womanist." Katie's reply, as I recall, was to tell her not to do it, to stop being an all-too-typical white person, grabbing for herself whatever seemed valuable in someone else's tradition. "Womanist" is a term that comes out of the African American experience; leave it there!

Similarly, it is tempting to lift up and celebrate Hagar, now that Williams has drawn our attention to her, and forget about Sarah, the slave woman's master, but our task is precisely to remember Sarah in all of her ecosocial location as well as to recognize that Hagar also is part of the story, a part we had ignored.[5]

How often have we white feminists quoted Audre Lorde and Alice Walker as if they were ours, ignoring their ecosocial locations and experiences? How often have we assumed commonality and ignored difference?

At the same time, I think the relationship should be more complex than a simple "hands off" and a stance of respect suggest. As others' traditions become available to us, we should be open to them and learn from them. They give us other perspectives on ourselves and allow us to be changed by them. When I read Williams's discussion of Hagar, for instance, I have to rethink how I thought about Sarah as a slave owner. When I read about the lives of African American women, I have to challenge central dimensions of ecofeminist theory about the relationship between women and the natural world. As a result of the work several of us have done with indigenous people in the Northeast, I have become much more aware of the importance of ritual in our lives, for instance, and of how different a ritual orientation to the world is from an essentially calendar orientation. Indigenous spirituality has also helped me think through Christian dualism toward a nondualistic construction of reality.

Reading Jewish feminists constantly challenges me about the anti-Semitism I grew up with and have internalized. I have had radically to rethink Jesus, my use of Scripture, and Christological beliefs. This is a journey that I feel I have barely begun. Looking back, I think almost all of my religious and theological education has assumed an anti-Semitic context and condition. White Christians simply assumed that the various Christian approaches to the Bible were the only ones that counted. As Plaskow wrote, "For two thousand years, Christian interpreters have read Hebrew Scripture in a way that renders invisible both Israelite religion and the subsequent history of rabbinic interpretation."[6]

Respecting the stories and experiences of women of cultures different from my own also can open my eyes to new resources in my own culture. This has particularly been the case in my working with indigenous women and men. I have come to look for and find, in European traditions, positive human–natural world relationships and constructions that I had not seen before. And this has helped me appreciate not only difference but also commonality, without reducing either to the other. These relationships have existed within "pagan" European traditions and also within Christian ones.

Reading and hearing such stories broadens and deepens my own identity. In this country, our histories are related; they have interacted and shaped one another from the beginning of white presence here. The experiences, stories, and traditions of people of color become part of my memories and thus part of the heritage that connects us in the past as well as the present. Sethe's life, in Toni Morrison's *Beloved*, is now indelibly a part of my history as an American.[7] I am threaded to the lives of black people in this country in a way in which I was not before I read *Beloved*. Working with miigm'agan, a MicMac woman, and gkisedtanamoogk, her Wampanoag husband, has shaped and reshaped my past, present, and future and, I hope, theirs. My ecosocial location, my privileged vantage point, now has breaches that cannot be restored. I am threaded to their lives as well as to the lives of African Americans. My heritage now has a richer texture, a breathtaking pain and beauty, that connects, humbles, and amazes me.

Listening to the stories of women from cultures other than my own also increases the depth of my understanding about "the human condition," the demonic and the exalted, and the complex—horrible and gracious—expression of that condition as displayed by members of my own culture. That deepening subtly shapes and continues to inform my beliefs, actions, and identity. Again, *Beloved* continues to hold before me such a prism.

Finally, feminists and womanists in these other traditions are themselves critically examining their own traditions and are developing new theologies, ethics, liturgies, and understandings of the church. There is profound work going on in all of these traditions, including reclaiming from the indigenous past those dimensions that have been ignored, devalued, and/or corrupted by Christianity. I am most familiar with the work of womanists, but that of *mujeristas* and Asian women is also deeply exciting to me.

In light of the complexities raised here, I want to make several methodological suggestions. One, as Plaskow identified in her essay, is that we should recognize that whatever differences or commonalities we may be exploring, they come from different traditions.

Second, however, we should allow our theory to be shaped by both the differences and the commonalities. The boundaries are permeable, not in order to exploit but in order to be changed—as theory and as a person—and in order to be held accountable to one another.

When I turn to European traditions, some of which reflect my own ethnic heritage, those boundaries get fuzzier, but they still exist. These traditions include women mystics, women hymn-writers, women authors of popular religious writings, and women's organizations and movements led or largely peopled by women—from early church times to the present. They also include European goddess traditions. Even these traditions belong to times and places different from our own, and those differences must be respected. Their usefulness as a resource in constructing a post-Christendom white feminist theology is real but limited.

Certainly it is important to reconstruct our religious and/or European American women's past. Finding that women were actors in the early church helps create space for me in the contemporary church and encourages me to continue the tradition of leadership. My heart is stirred as I meditate on the woman who anointed Jesus, for instance, or on Mary Magdalene or on the many anonymous women who helped found the church.

I also gain strength and inspiration from the ever-widening company of women being rediscovered throughout the history of the church. I see a stream of theologians, activists, worshipers, and workers through the centuries: women of deep faith who, through their presence and prayers and physical labor, quietly enabled the church to survive; women mystics who were also artists, scientists, administrators, and statespeople and who helped shape medieval culture and institutions; women protesters who challenged those institutions and created new ones; women who were silenced, oppressed, and abused by the church; women martyrs who fought and died in the struggle to create a more just church and world; women I knew in person—Rachel Henderlite, Elinor Curry, Valerie Russell, and many others—who inspired, challenged, and affirmed me to continue the struggle and live a vision. I live with a sense of their presence that is almost palpable. I stand with them. I realize that I don't identify with male actors and thinkers in these European and European American traditions; they are not the cloud of witnesses. The women are; they bear me along, and I am accountable to them.

So, recovering this heritage is critically important for me, but the contexts and conditions of these women were, to more or less significant degrees, also different from mine. I cannot make those who weren't into twentieth-century feminists or environmentalists. And if I turn to these women as resources, I need to acknowledge the differences and allow them to exist and allow myself to be shaped by them as well as to draw on them. I love reading the works of some of the women mystics, for instance, but I also have serious problems with some of their theologies, particularly their emphasis on unity and harmony.

When I first turned to European goddess traditions, the differences jumped out. Socialized to think of them as "fertility" religions, a label that devalued them (and my body and the earth), I wondered how I could relate positively to them. Now, I am angered by the ease with which so many women appropriate goddesses and ignore the differences of context and condition. So the both-and kind of response that I have been delineating holds for my relationship to these traditions just as it does for the ones discussed above.

We exploit goddess traditions and the women who are a part of those traditions when we take them out of their historical contexts and make them over into our image for commercial purposes—goddess coloring books, for instance. I think this kind of trivialization of religions that nurtured and empowered people for thousands of years reflects the still-present colonization of women's minds—our internalization of our own trivialization. We also exploit these religions when we make goddess figures into Pre-Raphaelite stereotypes, with long flowing hair and slender youthful bodies. From the information we have, they were imaged wholly differently!

And yet, we desperately need to recover these traditions and learn from them, as we should learn from womanist and other traditions. Carol Christ once wrote an essay entitled "Why Women Need the Goddess."[8] I would modify that title because I think it is not women in general but rather white feminists and white women who need not *the* goddess but rather the goddess traditions. The theological usefulness of those traditions is limited, but within those limits it is extremely important. So . . . "Why White, Christian, Middle-Class, Feminist Women Need Goddess Traditions" (not all reasons will equally apply to all such women).

I believe that we need immersion in goddess traditions, not simply an intellectual acquaintance with them. We need to pray to specific goddesses, to celebrate goddess rituals, to be surrounded by stories and images of goddesses. First, immersion in a such a woman-centered universe offers a concrete opportunity to experience our bodies, to experience a construction of reality that is female. It challenges us to affirm our bodies and to become more aware of just how gendered our understanding of deity is. Protestations to the contrary notwithstanding, I think that masculine and male imagery has become a part of God's *being* in the dominant Christian tradition. To challenge masculine images is to challenge dominant Protestant Christianity at its very heart. Further, to affirm such images is to affirm something not quite respectable—something make-believe, silly, undignified. It is interesting how we can call on a Father God in all seriousness but snicker or feel uncomfortable when we call on Diana. Sensitivity to this discrepancy can help us to explore the deeply ingrained biases—about women and body—that have become a part of us, that still reside in the house of our spirit.

Second, such immersion can help us to understand incarnation. This may sound odd, since Christian theology is rooted in incarnation, but it is rooted in a doctrine about incarnation, not necessarily in a felt understanding, an experience of the sacred as incarnate. It is difficult to name goddesses, to think of goddesses, without thinking of female bodies. The images are concrete, embodied images. They are sacred power in female forms—and a whole range of forms at that.

Third, immersion in goddess traditions offers a wide range of female images for the sacred: Hecate, Artemis, Isis; the little, fat figures with huge breasts and thighs; Asherah, or Astarte, whom the biblical God warred against and whose land was conquered. There are the birds and bulls and snakes that accompany various goddesses in story and drawing. There are sexuality and fertility; there are emotionality and rationality; there are grief and joy and resentment and revenge. These images challenge our abstractions; they surround us with plurality, richness, and sensuousness.

They also challenge our Western, Victorian notions of *feminine* and *privileged white womanhood.* When I call on Artemis, for instance, I call on power that can be creative and/or destructive, forces that aren't and can't be domesticated. Artemis was "a virgin goddess whose domain was . . . the wild places, mountains and springs. As such, her primary appeal was freedom and independence from others."[9] She was the protector of hunters *and* young animals, of infants and their mothers; she was also the one who killed mothers in childbirth.

And finally, immersion within a goddess-constructed reality can put us imaginatively in touch with the women of the early church, as well as with the people Israel conquered. Many early Gentile Christian women came from goddess worship into the church and brought their practices and constructs with them. In her groundbreaking study of women's worship in Philippi, for instance, Valerie Abrahamsen has demonstrated something of the variety and richness of women worshipers. They were artists, priests, and contributors to women's religious sites and practices. They performed rituals that supported both women's lives and concerns and the welfare of the city itself. And they brought those skills, practices, and roles into the church. Baptism, for instance, may have been initiated by those women, although the writers of the Bible trace it to John's baptism of Jesus.[10]

Connecting us to a more distant past, participation in goddess rituals can remind us that Asherah was worshiped on the hillsides of Israel and Judas when the Hebrews came into that land. Her sacred groves were cut down, her priests executed, her rituals proscribed. She was denounced by the very prophets we honor for their commitment to justice and to right relations with God.

This kind of imaginative reconstruction of our past helps us to claim our whole past—its ambiguity and complexity—or at least more of it than we have been given by the fathers. We are not the inheritors of a thin line of biblical and Christian history, particularly its dominant version. We are the inheritors of messy struggles— cultural, political, and theological—among pagan, biblical, and postbiblical actors and ideas. Such a multifaceted tradition helps us to locate biblical documents more accurately in the midst of those struggles and at the same time gives us many more resources for reconstructing theology.

A CIRCLE OF STONES

To use a pagan image, I lay down a circle of stones to mark my sacred circle. The stones represent where I stand, descriptively and normatively, for exploring a post-Christendom Christian feminist theology. The stones are my own location and the various locations of the voices of other women, of men, and of the natural world; an understanding of Jesus as one who pointed to and lived out of a commitment to God and who was bringing into existence a new society of justice, healing, compassion, and friendship; a series of ethical principles for living and thinking today that is a continuation of the vision that Jesus shared with his people in his day; and an openness, variously expressed, toward a range of Christian and non-Christian traditions, including goddess traditions.

The circle is sure but fragile. Other stones can be selected. Stones within it can be replaced by ones of richer hues and more dramatic shapes. Stones can be added or omitted. They can be turned differently or placed in a different location. My theological method, in other words, involves both an ongoing conversation and a commitment.

3

THEOLOGY OF GOD
AND THE WORLD

You have made us for ourselves, and our hearts are restless until they find their rest in You.

—*St. Augustine, paraphrase from* Confessions

I call you sister,
I call you mother,
I call you friend,
I call you lover.
    I turn around and you're standing there;
    I dream a dream and you greet me there.
You are beauty. You are power.
    You are the rainbow and the shower.
Mountain, wind and fire and sea
    In everything and deep . . . in me.
        Brigit McCallum, "I Call You Sister"

In this chapter, I will begin to develop a theology, an understanding of God, that has Christian feminist truth in our journey toward a post-Christendom church and life. I will do this by exploring a number of contributions to the construction. As I have reiterated, this in no way means that all voices are equal. It means that the influences on and resources for me are many and that it is better to be aware of them than blind to them and also to appropriate what is useful without exploiting the culture from which the useful comes.

AFFIRMING DIMENSIONS OF MY PAST

In constructing theology, I acknowledge and still assume as valid, if relative, certain dimensions from my past. I grew up in the church. There I developed a faith that

53

was focused on God rather than Christ, and there I began a lifelong love affair with this God, who remained ambiguous but compelling. I also responded early to those strains in my religious ethos that emphasized concern for the welfare of others. At the same time, for most of my life, I have experienced myself as on the margins of the church. Theologically, I questioned everything I heard; personally, with some significant exceptions, I felt I had little or no voice.

As a result of meeting Rachel Henderlite when I was in Richmond, I discovered the writings of H. Richard Niebuhr, with whom she had studied at Yale. With Niebuhr and Martin Buber, I found insights and themes that remain a positive legacy for me. Both men, for instance, described relationality as constitutive of our existence. We are beings-in-relation. Understanding ourselves as relational as a basic description bypasses the body/soul dualism and individualism of so much of traditional theology. Further, relationality does not mean mutuality; relationality can be expressed in different ways. For Buber, for instance, it can be either an I-Thou relationship or an I-It one, and the one typically becomes the other. Either may be appropriate, depending on the situation. For Niebuhr, the self can also respond in different ways to its reality of relatedness; it can, for instance, respond in defensiveness or anxiety; or it can respond in trust and openness.

A second important theme for both men is revelation. In relationships, selves reveal, speak, communicate, and show forth who they are. Selves can also be objectified, studied, ignored, and stereotyped, of course. But what matters for both men is the knowledge we gain of ourselves and others through self-disclosure, through revelation.

A third important theme is that God is an integral part of our relatedness. According to Buber, "Every particular *Thou* is a glimpse through to the eternal *Thou*."[1] According to Niebuhr, "My response to every particular action takes the form of response also to the One that is active in it."[2] For Buber, God is met in the depth of the *between,* in each encounter. For Niebuhr also, God is active in each encounter but beyond all encounters. For both, therefore, we meet and respond to God in the concreteness of our lives, not in trying to flee it.

At the same time, there is an important difference between the theologies of the two men. For Buber, a major significance of this understanding of humanity and God is that any specific relationship can become sacramental. By being there, by being genuinely "attentive," only by being there for another person can one meet the eternal Thou. Another self cannot be simply a means to that end. For Niebuhr, however, our specific relationships are relativized in their significance as we respond to God in them. Niebuhr's concern is with the temptation to give ultimate value to the creation. Buber's is with restoring real respect for all created beings.

Finally, an ethic of responsiveness, particularly as Niebuhr delineates it in *The Responsible Self,* has been a major legacy for me. This involves an effort to understand the moral life not just or primarily as obedience to laws or to God or as moving toward a goal or end. It recognizes that we are not isolated individuals, always standing at some atomistic moral crossroads with a decision about which way to go. Rather, it recognizes that we are enmeshed in all kinds of relationships with responsibilities, emotions, roles, histories, and values and that our decisions are like sentences in an ongoing conversation. We try to speak appropriately (Niebuhr's phrase is "fittingly"). But whatever we may say at one point may or may not be appropriate, or fitting, in the next paragraph.

An ethic of response and responsiveness is an alternative to the dogmatic and controlling character of so much of traditional Christian ethics, particularly European ethics. Ethics of obedience reflect a hierarchical paradigm of society-reality, in which those below should obey those above, whether the latter be God, the government, one's mind-spirit, men, or white people. An ethic of obedience is also an ethic of control, control of those below by those above. This character of traditional Christian ethics is seen most clearly in the areas of sexuality and bodily existence. But it is seen also in other areas, for although the claim that "we must obey God rather then 'men'" has been a part of the dominant traditions, the overarching norms have dictated obedience to those in power and thus at best allowed only some reform of the status quo rather than significant theological or social change.

Both Niebuhr and Buber, however, broke from that tradition and sketched a significantly different way of being human and responsible in the world. Indeed, from the perspective of relatedness, one could critique hierarchical patterns as broken or distorted relationships, not as the normative pattern. Similarly, an ethic of obedience can be understood as one response, but one that is difficult to maintain in an I-Thou relationship (Buber) or that is inappropriate in many situations (Niebuhr).

This kind of ethic is a resource for feminist ethics, I believe. It also, to some extent, anticipates some significant feminist themes. With the publication of *In a Different Voice,* for instance, Carol Gilligan and others have attempted to delineate an ethic of responsiveness as distinctively feminine.[3] And I recall sitting in a graduate seminar shortly after the posthumous publication of *The Responsible Self,* which a faculty member critiqued as "too feminine." Even though I had no conscious feminist vocabulary at that time (1963–64), I objected to the devaluation explicit in that designation, and I remember being angry about the faculty member's negative connotation of the word "feminine."

A major theme in Niebuhr's writing is his emphasis on monotheism, indeed radical monotheism. To understand God as radically monotheistic, as the one beyond the many, means that God cannot be identified with, much less equated with, any particular cause, value, or loyalty. God's nature, will, and activity may be revealed in those but are not identified as any of those. To speak of God as radically monotheistic is to speak of "an infinite center of value" rather than specific finite centers of value. God is not to be identified with the "Contract with America" or feminism or liberation of the poor or any other particular commitments, however good any of us may judge them.

Further, according to Niebuhr, God's presence is experienced typically as hostile power. God is experienced as the ultimate limitation to our existence and causes. God is that power of the universe—other than me and us—that eventually defeats our purposes. For Niebuhr, the basic theological question is not "Does God exist?" but "Is God good?" It is only as God is experienced in Jesus Christ that the inimical power can be known as good, although even that revelation is as much a transformation of our understanding of good as it is a positive communication of goodness.

> Yet the goodness that shines upon us through the moment of revelation is not the glory or the goodness we had expected in our thought about deity. . . . We sought a good to love and were found by a good that loved us. . . . Here is goodness that empties itself, and makes itself of no reputation, a goodness that is all outgoing, reserving nothing for itself, yet having all things. So we must begin to rethink all our definitions of deity and convert all our worship and our prayers. Revelation is not the development and not the elimination of our natural religion; it is the revolution of the religious life.[4]

The relativity and the transformation of our lives are important and valuable, but the emphasis, which Niebuhr inherits from the tradition, on the sovereign oneness of God remains problematic for feminists seeking an alternative understanding—one more gracious and just—of power. As Hannah Arendt, another who has deeply influenced my thinking, pointed out in *On Violence,* the power of the one *against* (Niebuhr's word is "beyond") the many is absolute tyranny.[5] Regardless of the preposition, it is still the power of one; it is not shared. The persistence of this legacy is dangerous.

It is important, thus, to recognize that both Niebuhr and Buber suggest alternative ways of being human and of being responsible, ways that are at least consistent with feminist values and politics. Although there are certainly dimensions of their thinking that I reject, there are also important resources in the dominant traditions of my past, and I remain indebted to them, even to some extent to my conservative Presbyterian past. That past has to some extent shaped me, for better and worse, and as I construct a post-Christendom Christian feminist understanding of God, I will build on it as well as depart from it significantly.

TOWARD A FEMINIST REIMAGING AND
RECONSTRUCTION OF GOD

Feminist-womanist theologians have been imaging God and reconstructing theology now for nearly three decades. As I reflect on their writings, on feminist social analysis and the connection between social hierarchies, oppression, and violence, and on the ways in which traditional European American theological constructions inevitably support hierarchical social patterns, the most fundamental issue that emerges for me is the question of power. That is, how should we understand sacred power?

Susan Thistlethwaite summarized the issue well: "The most common model of God's power in Christian history is the absolute violence of the One Against the All. Hannah Arendt has written, 'The extreme form of power is All against One, the extreme form of violence is One against All.'"[6] Similarly, Elizabeth Johnson has written, "The idea of the impassible, omnipotent God . . . is morally intolerable."[7]

In reimaging and redefining the power of God, feminists-womanists, along with many others, begin with a model of relationality and understand God's power in relationship. Thistlethwaite, for instance, defines that power as solidarity, though she does not really elaborate on that definition.[8]

Carter Heyward, however, devotes much of her writing to this issue. She defines God as the power "with and by which . . . we are able to nurture relationships as resources of growth as cocreative women and men."[9] She adds, "God is our power in mutual relation."[10] God is the power of the relationship. God is not a partner in a relationship but is the power of the between. We participate in this power and act to cocreate friendship and justice in the world. Heyward, like Mary Daly earlier, thinks of God as a verb more than as a noun.

In *Womanist Justice, Womanist Hope,* Emily Townes addresses this issue implicitly in her discussion of the suffering of African American women.[11] Following Audre Lorde, she distinguishes between pain and suffering. Suffering is an endless reliving of pain, an acceptance of pain. Pain is a terrible reality that must be named and challenged. For Townes, God does not will or allow suffering. The empty cross symbolizes God's victory over injustice and therefore demands and empowers a suffering people not to suffer but to act, not simply to endure the pain but to name it and its sources and challenge it.[12]

Townes's discussion removes suffering from the will of a God who is good and powerful, and although she does not say so, I think she implicitly also rejects the idea that God is all-powerful, as dominant Christianity has understood God. She refers to James Cone in a critical passage: "Cone admits that there is no historical evidence that God liberates Black people from oppression. Instead, African-American Christians turn to Jesus as God's active presence in their lives. This Jesus helps them know that they were not created for bondage but for freedom."[13]

Delores Williams does not directly address the issue of God and power. Implicitly, however, she seems to reject a hierarchical understanding, in her critique of black liberation theology with its emphasis on the Exodus event, in her description of God's activity as solidarity with Hagar in the wilderness, and in her identification of Jesus' mission as a ministerial vision. In the liberation emphasis on the Exodus, she notes, black theologians ignore the violence and the ultimate genocide that "God is supposed to have sanctioned."[14] Similarly, in her discussion of Hagar and God, she cites God's announcement of Ishmael's birth and his promise in Genesis 16:11–12 and then observes: "The promise assures survival, and the birth announcement forecasts the strategy that will be necessary for survival and for obtaining a quality of life. . . . [Ishmael] will be able to help create and protect the quality of life he and his mother, Hagar, will later develop in the desert."[15]

And Jesus' ministerial vision is a ministry of teaching, touching, healing, compassion, and challenge. Further, and equally important, if it is Jesus' life that is redemptive, and not his death on the cross, then the power expressed in his life reveals the nature of God's power, which is not the power of an absolute God sacrificing God's self/son for us.

These writers, as well as Niebuhr and Buber and feminist social analysts, provide a basis for constructing my own understanding of reality and God's power. Specifically I wish to construct an understanding of God as multiple dimensions of God as power in relation and as object of loyalty and love.

1. GOD AS RELATIONAL POWER(S)

As I wrote above, God does not exist alone; God exists *in relation*. God is power in relationship. God is not a partner in a relationship; God is the power of the between. God is present always, closer to us than our own heart. To use a biblical image, God is Emmanuel. I think it is Jay McDonald who wrote somewhere that creation ex nihilo is the ultimate male fantasy.

Understanding God as power in relationship means that creatures have (and should have, when it is denied them by others) power. As we, other animals, and even plants shape one another, as we become in and through our relationships, we mediate sacred power. The power of God is the within of our actions.

One of the profound implications of this understanding is that God is deeply affected by what creatures do; God can be strengthened, changed, scarred, and/or diminished by what creatures do. Our relationships are fundamentally shaped by historical patterns of amazing grace, beauty, and oppression, of terror, callousness, brutality, and hate. In such patterns, the power to nurture growth, for instance, is severely warped, or it struggles against other, negative dimensions of relationships. And when I think of the millions of people who have been destroyed, physically and/or emotionally, and of other millions of animals and plants, not to mention earth and air and water, I have to ask to what extent the power to nurture relationships, power that has existed in the relationships within which all that destruction has taken place, to what extent has that power been killed?

This question sends me deeper into the nature of God's power. Fundamental to any understanding of Christianity are the beliefs that God is good, that God is imaged in Jesus, that God seeks and accomplishes human salvation (well-being, health, communion with God and one another), and that God endures. These affirmations and the diversity of feminists' and womanists' insights about God's power suggest that I should not identify only one kind of power in relation as God. To do justice to both the Christian faith and the reality of our lives, I have identified six (and there are no doubt others): God is the power of survival, of solidarity, of liberation, of mutuality, of creativity, and of mystery. God is the powers that sustain, challenge, and struggle against unjust, demonic forces and that nurture growth, creativity, mutuality, and communion. God is the eternal wellspring of possibility and renewal, generating life in despair and transcending our most joyous vision.

Survival. The power to survive is perhaps the most widespread power in the universe. The poor and the oppressed learn how to survive. The abused woman learns to survive. The withered grass somehow manages to survive. The raccoon survives. Somehow they all draw on powers that enable them to continue, to adapt, to persist in living. God is that power, made available to them. The power to survive exists sometimes in the presence of others, who stand with those who are desperate. It is sometimes written in their hearts and genes. It is made available through a people's membership in a history of those who have survived.

We all live and seek to continue to live within limited possibilities, often extremely limited. The struggle to survive thus may well lead creatures to reject the norms and values of the dominant culture. So God is present in relationships in which gay and lesbian people are forced to lie, in which survivors of sexual abuse blot out dimensions of themselves and their past, and in which a child in the ghetto turns to drugs—all in order to survive.

The elites of this world also learn to survive. To put this in more traditional Christian religious language, God loves the CEO as well as the AFDC mother. God wants the continued existence and well-being of both, but what that means is quite different for each. The CEO may find life meaningless, but the sacred power to survive may be manifest as his heart tells him to abandon his little (or not so little) empire. He may be frightened by a threat to his empire in the form of a rebellion of workers, and the sacred power to survive may be made available to him in the voice of a friend who tells him to listen to those workers.

God as the power of survival is available to me. God wills my survival. I am not just an enemy or a victim or one of the oppressed or one of the oppressors. I am. I should live, and as I lay hold of the power of living, I try to carve out a space for myself even as I try to discern its limits.

God as the power to survive is present not only within human relationships but in all of life—in the rabbit and the eagle, the osprey and the mackerel. It is present in corn and "weeds" (plants that certain people have designated as worthless). Here, as in human relationships, this power is made available in relationships of protection and community as well as in innate messages written in heart, genes, and memories.

Solidarity. God is the power of solidarity. For many, this is Jesus' revelation of God—present, standing with the outcast and those on the margins of society. Solidarity enhances the possibilities of survival as people move from survival to challenge. Power is needed to survive, but a somewhat different kind of power is needed to protest and resist.

God as the power of solidarity exists as people come together to resist and/or push toward transformation of a society and relationships. Such power exists in anger, profound love, glimpses of alternative ways of being in the world, and unconditional commitment to stand with those who are oppressed. An individual may resist alone, in solidarity with him/herself. It is an act of integrity, of internal wholeness, an act in which the many dimensions of a self come together, and the person speaks with Luther, "Here I stand; I can do no other." But that action gains exponential power as others stand with the individual. The Montgomery bus boycott, the women at Greenham Commons, and the many less-dramatic "standing with" in the struggle for liberation and justice all represent the power of solidarity.

The power of solidarity is available to all people, but again, as with the power of survival, the ecosocial locations of people of varying elite status shape that power differently than do the ecosocial locations of the oppressed. Relatively speaking, the oppressed are more in touch with the power of solidarity than elites are. Nevertheless, God's power is available to both. As elites seek ways to use their power for justice for all, they open themselves to sources of strength and support within themselves. They also become more open to the support and strength of the others with whom they are beginning to stand. And one hopes that they will find themselves in church communities of solidarity and will eventually even be supported by those who are oppressed.

God as the power of solidarity is available to me. I am a member of various communities and groups that seek to stand with others, that seek to be in alliance with others. Within those groups and from others, I also need and seek solidarity. I need people to be there for me as I struggle toward wholeness and responsibility. I need to share my visions of a just society, of the new creation. I need support and encouragement to give voice to my insights and questions, my fears and hopes. I need expressions of solidarity from womanists and from feminist women of color, not to reassure me that I am right but to strengthen and deepen the resistance, to challenge and support me, to clarify what we are about as we work on our own necessary agendas and on common ones. I deeply value the possibilities of the alliance work that has been established here in Maine. Through these groups, as well as through other activist relationships and friendships, God as the power of solidarity strengthens and supports me.

God as the power of solidarity exists in the relationships of all living beings, not only the human, but I have little knowledge of how that power works. That ignorance may be due to my thinking that solidarity requires more intentionality than survival, and I have a difficult time ascribing intentionality to most of the rest of creation. At the same time, in terms of effects, or consequences, I can see resistance at work in the natural world. The floods in the Midwest in the summer of 1993 are a good example. The floods in effect were the waters fighting back, reclaiming floodplains and, in so doing, reestablishing a healthy ecosystem, one in which people and nature can live together, not one in which nature must be subdued and controlled for humans to do whatever they wish.

There are many such examples of nature "fighting back," although too few people seem to be heeding the protest. Earthquakes are one example, many forms of cancer are another, and I sometimes wonder about other diseases. To what extent are diseases a result of the human destructive intervention into the natural world?

Liberation. God is the power of liberation. This has become the most celebrated understanding of God in contemporary theology and has sparked widespread movements and theologies. Liberation is setting one free to become what one can become and to exercise power in shaping one's life and the lives of others. Liberation always is individual and communal; one doesn't become free alone.

Liberation is the movement from bondage and protest toward justice. It is an ongoing activity and transformation, not a once-and-for-all event. And it is a struggle; like a blade of grass trying to grow through cement, the power of liberation must crack systems that have been cemented in place for centuries. God as the power of survival and solidarity may be at work in people's lives for decades before the power of liberation is experienced.

As the movement from bondage, liberation is not simply freedom to do whatever one wants but is freedom toward justice—freedom in community to become whole and healthy and to exercise power for living well together and shaping a sufficient and sustainable future. Liberation not only is freedom from the oppressor-oppressive systems we live in but also is freedom for new systems, ones that celebrate health and the development of one's skills and interests. Since power is essential to health and growth, shared power is the taproot of the new creation.

Like the other powers of God, the power of liberation can be experienced by all of creation. As ecosystems lose their complex balance and flexibility, as they become unhealthy, there is change until either they die or a new health is established.

A part of the human task is to locate the social-justice liberation movement within this larger ecological liberation movement. This task requires radically different ways of thinking about justice issues, some of which I will address in the next two chapters. What is important here is to understand that as we work for liberation, if we can be in alliance, in solidarity, we can be open to all kinds of new insights and inspirations about how we can best live with one another and with the rest of creation on this globe.

The power of liberation has been imaged in many ways. In biblical tradition, the Exodus and the Jesus stories have been the most prominent and normative. As I think about liberation, I find myself tempted to use another image also, one that Niebuhr drew on often—that of God as enemy—although Niebuhr's use of the image is different from mine. For Niebuhr, God is the enemy of our "natural" selves; God is the absolute power that defeats our dreams, the object of our anxieties and the end of our existence. God is transformed into friend as we meet God in Jesus Christ. In contrast, when I think of God as enemy, I think as a privileged Christian. God is the enemy of my social security (speaking metaphorically more than literally, although the fact that I can draw even an exceedingly modest social security from the government is a privilege not shared by all). God is the enemy in that my heart and mind must continue to undergo conversion. It is a conversion to a vision of justice and welfare for all creatures, a vision that includes to some extent a changed way of living for me—a change that I will see as a loss as well as an improvement.

Mutuality. From Buber's chance encounter with a stranger on a park bench, to Vincent Harding's experience of eye contact with a white southern city councilman in the 1960s (a contact that briefly transcended their opposition), to passionate embrace, to mystical communion with God—we all experience the sacred power of mutuality.[16] In mutual relation, we are open to one another, bare. In mutual relation, we journey beyond the facades that each of us wears and move into our hearts. The more fully mutual we are, the more we open our body-spirit selves and allow the other to be open to us in all our complexity and ambiguity. Mutual relation is the relation of equality, vulnerability, and trust par excellence.

Mutual relation is deeply personal, although it can be tantalizingly and breathtakingly brief. We all experience mutuality; we all need it, and we all long for it. It is perhaps one of the most intrinsically meaningful experiences and sustainable relationships available to human beings. It is also the nurturing soil for individual growth and for caring commitment to the well-being of others. For many people, mutual relation is experienced briefly and/or is sustained and/or is expressed in genital sexual activities, but this is certainly not true of everyone. For whatever reasons, sex can be frightening, terrifying, anxious, boring, or mechanical, serving as an escape or as an exercise in control or dependency. Mutuality may not involve physical contact—that is, touch—at all. But it is, as Lorde, Heyward, and others have written so powerfully and eloquently, the power of eros, the sacred power that flows through the world.

Most of us probably find that need and longing deeply met in mutual relation with other people. Some of us may find it in mutual relation with other beings. I think we—all of us humans and perhaps *all* creatures—need and long for it with God; we long for mutual relation with the universe. This is the peace that passes understanding, the mystical communion, the sense of being at one with all that is. We become so deeply connected to the powers that swirl throughout life that we experience this sense of "at homeness." We have tapped into some reservoir or well-spring of eros; we glimpse the reality of what Augustine described when he wrote that our end is the love and enjoyment of God and of one another in God.

The power of mutual relation is deeply personal, but it has profound social implications as well. One is that it is possible to move from a personal experience of mutuality to the realization that all people long for mutual relation, to understand this from within, so to speak, and thus to begin to critique one's participation in systems that throw up obstacles or deny mutuality. Mutual relation can become a touchstone or an ongoing conversion in one's heart and mind toward resistance, healing, and transformation. As I write this, I am thinking primarily of elites and of those of us who share some of their privileges. But it is true of any of us. The power of mutuality can be a sharp sword that slices through the social and conceptual barriers of injustice and oppression.

An important way to move toward mutual relation is through forgiveness. We ask for forgiveness in worship and prayer. Forgiveness is breaking the chains of the past, starting fresh, and initiating a new kind of action that invites a new response. We need forgiveness: we need to ask for it and to grant it. God is here. Let us open ourselves to the power of mutual relation. I speak here, as I have said elsewhere, primarily to other white feminist Christians (but I extend the invitation to anyone). Forgiveness does not replace anger or fear or other responses to the world. They are all appropriate and necessary. Let's just add forgiveness to the list.

Further, it is critical to create institutional patterns and expectations of behavior that nurture mutuality rather than hierarchy and violence, stereotype and facade. This will mean changing the values that shape and guide institutional behavior, role definitions, and typical ways of interacting with one another. For instance, we need to replace debate with discussion, one-upmanship with cooperation, an emphasis on punitive measures with one on positive encouragements, dishonesty with honesty, and of course, ladders of power and authority with circles of broadly shared power and authority.

Above, I referred to creatures other than human beings. Here I want to explore further the power of mutual relation in their lives. It seems obvious that in much of the natural world, the power of mutual relation exists as it does between human beings and other creatures. Buber thought an I-Thou relationship was possible with a tree, and perhaps it swirls through all relationships. I expect that what scientists have called "instinct," which is a social construction of dominant white males whose culture has valued reason as a human (i.e., male) characteristic, is a complex phenomenon that may include dimensions of the power of survival and of mutual relation. Earlier European social constructions visualized the world as an organism in which each component was alive and interacting with the others. At the same time, indigenous constructions on this continent visualized the world as spirit-filled. Plants and animals had their own *Manito*—life force, power. All of these constructions are much more consistent with biblical images of trees clapping their hands and of the earth reveling in praise of God.

Creativity. A fundamental Christian affirmation is that God is creator. I have chosen the term "creativity" to stress the ongoing activity of creation. God is the power of creation, the power of creativity that is expressed throughout the world. The world is both created and creator.

In a relational understanding of reality, creation does not occur out of nothing but rather is a participant in its own ongoing birthing and developing. The artist sculpts a form out of a piece of wood, transforming the wood. At the same time, the viewer *sees* something new—not only an object but something about light or composition or color that delights or disturbs.

Art is one expression of this sacred power of creativity. There are many, many others. It exists in the daily miracles of healing and transformation, in making bread and love, in building houses that shelter and delight.

We create and are created by others as we become, as we fashion ourselves (and are fashioned) out of the raw materials of our histories and ecosocial locations, our genes and the people in our lives, our experiences and the longings of our hearts. Where we are open to the power of mutual relation, to survival, to solidarity, and to liberation, creativity can take incredibly and miraculously beautiful forms—forms that may simultaneously surprise and shock or repel. Where, or insofar as, those powers are blocked, our creativity can produce clichéd, twisted, or even demonic forms. Fortunately, since creativity is ongoing, further change is possible, however stubbornly it may be resisted.

Creation is also discovery. When I write I make something; I also discover new insights. As we create ourselves and one another, as we create new worlds, we discover truths or principles to guide our further creation. We discover mistakes; we discover new possibilities that we had not dreamed of earlier.

Each artist also creates in a distinctive way. She or he leaves some kind of stamp on the creation that identifies it as this particular artist's work. In creating, we leave distinctive stamps on the world. Unfortunately, we have too many terrible examples of this. But many of us are grateful for the people in our lives who have left their stamp on us and on the world we seek to fashion.

The power of creativity exists throughout the world. It exists in the emergence of new ecosystems, new species, new individuals. It exists daily—in the curl of a wave, the soft sleekness of a cat's fur, the glory of lupine. In writing this, I am reminded of Annie Dillard's observation after she rounded the corner of a building to see a mockingbird plummet toward the ground and then, just before crashing, spread its wings and fly off: grace and beauty exist, but we must be there to see them.

As I think of images of the power of creativity, God as artist comes to mind, but there are many others. A woman giving birth is an image both of creativity and of the power of mutual relation; it could also be an image of the power of survival.

Mystery. God is mystery. Behind, beneath, beyond, there is more. There could be no creativity without mystery—no miracle, no real renewal. We can never plumb the depths of even someone with whom we are in intimate contact. I am incapable of plumbing my own depths. Every once in a while I surprise myself. Sometimes I am distressed or shocked, and at other times I am delighted and impressed.

Living on the coast of Maine, I often see seals, and I am always struck by the luminous intelligence of their eyes. I have had the same experience with dolphins and even to some extent with my Siamese cats. They *look* at me; they seem to delight in making eye contact and holding it. With all three—seals, dolphins, and Siamese cats—I experience intelligence, recognition, and a depth I cannot penetrate. There is mystery, openness but still mystery. And sometimes I imagine God as a sleek, talkative, beautiful Siamese cat.

I believe that mystery is the beyond of all creatures, even those in whom I personally don't find much depth—black flies, for instance. I swat them rather than try to look into their tiny eyes. But I have no doubt that sacred power is manifest in their relationships with other black flies as well as with other beings in their world.

There is mystery, out of whose depths we come and to which we go. There is mystery, but it is not a void; it is the source out of which stream the power of mutual relation, of creativity, of solidarity, of liberation, and of survival. Put in more traditional religious language, God is eternal, and God is creator. God's love is boundless and unconditional.

To understand God in terms of relational powers fundamentally challenges the hierarchical and authoritarian concepts of much of the dominant strands of traditional Christianity. God is still transcendent, that is, beyond any particular relationship, indeed is a dimension of all relationships and of the universe itself. God is still immanent—that is, present—in each relationship of my life. But God's power is not a power-over. God is not a king or a CEO who orders subjects to do "his" bidding. God is not a despot, albeit a benevolent one.

Rather, God streams throughout the universe, present in all relationships, increased as creatures work together for justice; increased as power is shared so that all can survive and move toward their own and one another's well-being. "In everything and deep . . . in me."

Does this understanding mean that God is limited? Yes and no. Yes, God is limited if we begin with the oppressive understanding of power as absolute, over all others. Any reduction of this kind of power is then seen as limited. No, if we begin with a different definition of power. Then, God's power is strengthened, increased in relationship, or it can be. The key word for me is "interdependent" rather than "limited—or unlimited."

To understand God as the power to survive, to challenge and resist, and to grow toward the fullness of life is to affirm that the realm of God is present as a possibility and, to some extent, an actuality. As Christians, we still must bear witness to both the possibility and the actuality and must work toward its fuller expression in the world now. To affirm real freedom in the world is to acknowledge that bearing witness is becoming part of a real, ongoing struggle. Our individual and group responsibilities and contributions will vary as we understand our different movements in and from our current ecosocial locations in light of our visions of "the kingdom" or, the image I prefer, "new creation." In those movements, we will stumble, fall, and fail one another. My hope is that we will also help to sustain and inspire one another: may the power of God be real in our lives!

2. GOD AS OBJECT OF LOYALTY AND LOVE

In Christian tradition and in everyday language, the concept of *god* includes both ultimacy and value. I reflected a part of the idea of ultimacy in the above discussion of mystery. Here I wish to construct an understanding of God as ultimate value. In doing so, I am indebted to a diverse group that includes H. Richard Niebuhr, James Gustafson, St. Augustine, and other Christian men and women who have placed faithfulness to God over conformity to any political, social, or religious status quo.

All have understood God as that which relativizes our loyalties, our values. "God has made us for himself and our hearts are restless until they find their rest in God," Augustine wrote. In our restlessness, we pursue God in money, patriotism, and other "gods," seeking security and peace. But a relationship with God transcends all of these and dramatically qualifies our love of any of them.

Others have expressed this transcendent loyalty in terms of action: "we must obey God rather than any human authority." God, not human institutions or individuals, is sovereign. For slaves, to know God as sovereign meant that white people were not God. Obedience to God has led to protest and civil disobedience, to draft resistance and rebellion.

I find this concept of God as beyond all our specific loves and loyalties profoundly important. I think that a feminist understanding of God as beyond, as ultimate, should include at least three themes: of *all,* the whole; of loving commitment to each individual being in that whole; and of ultimate value. Our loyalty to God should mean that we are loyal to all people, the earth, and the future rather than to specific people, territories, and the past or present. Our loyalty to God should mean love of the enemy and commitment to the outcast, to those who may be opposed to us. Our loyalty to God should mean that any specific commitments are to be cherished *and also* located in a commitment to a larger whole. Thus our loyalty to specific causes of justice exists in a loyalty to the well-being of all.

Jesus echoes these themes over and over in his stories of neighborly love and his actions of healing. To affirm belief in the God of Hebrew, Jewish, and Christian traditions is to affirm belief in one who cares for and is concerned about all creatures, not simply those we are connected with. This affirmation makes us relate our particular concerns, issues, and causes to universal well-being, to a universal context of care, challenge, and conversion.

For me personally, this is the central affirmation I make when I use the word "God." I am saying in effect that I am standing in a universe in which every being is of worth, that my localized responsibilities and loves are related to a larger whole, and that there are sources of loving power at work with me (and against me) to seek the well-being of all. This affirmation demands that I work for justice *and* that the justice I seek for myself, for other women, and for those others with whom I am connected must exist in a universal circle of justice to all beings.

GENDER, IMAGES, AND NAMES OF GOD

Images have traditionally been a primary form of construction. In dominant expressions of Christianity, particularly in Protestantism, God has been imaged as absolute power and as sacrificial love (and/or as absolute power who sacrifices his son), as father and judge, as husband of Israel and liberator. Jesus has been imaged as Messiah/Christ and Emmanuel, lord and servant, husband of the church, son of God and God.

White feminists have sought both gender-inclusive and female-feminine images for God. God is mother as well as father, she as well as he. More recently there has been interest in Sophia, the Greek translation of the wisdom of God found in the Hebrew Scriptures and one of the major female images of God in the Bible. The most ambitious work to date on this image is Elizabeth Johnson's *She Who Is,* a study of the Trinity that begins with the Spirit as Sophia, moves to Jesus as Sophia incarnate, and then concludes with God as origin, imaged as birthing mother.[17]

I obviously agree that it is essential for us to image God in more than male and masculine language. Female images are important, and many are largely unexamined. In working with God as mother, Johnson emphasizes birthing images. After citing Isaiah's use of the image in "I will cry out like a woman in labor / I will gasp and pant," Johnson next wrote, "The loud birth cries evoke a God who is in hard labor, sweating, pushing with all her might to bring forth justice, the fruit of her love."[18] That is an image that evokes a kind of power radically different from the traditional power as control and decree.

But reliance on a few images, female as well as male ones, almost inevitably leads to reification and/or to support of injustice. When God is invoked or referred to only or primarily as mother or father, the temptation is to make God a mother or father. God becomes a supreme parent, garbed in the cultural characteristics and roles expected of parents. When this occurs, our theology implicitly supports hierarchy—one of the perpetual dependency of some human beings on others and one of humanity over the natural world. Further, mother images, as well as father images, can be negative for those who have been abused or abandoned by a parent. And so many families are so dysfunctional that parents may inadvertently reflect and/or sanction realities that many of us want to disavow.[19]

Indigenous people have regarded the earth as mother without necessarily organizing social relationships hierarchically or, so far as I know, questioning that image in light of negative parent-child relationships. In traditional indigenous societies, the nuclear family—and with it the parent-child relationship—is not the central or only familial unit. It may be that in societies or communities where there is more of an extended family unit, this preoccupation with parental images for the divine is simply less important.

But it is important for us to go beyond reliance on parental images for God. It is critically important to experiment with a whole range of different images that illumine dimensions of a feminist understanding and experience of the sacred. For instance, I would like to experiment with the use of a variety of names—YHWH, Isis, Elohim, Artemis, Sophia, Asherah, Astarte, Hecate, Bridget.[20] I prefer this to the use of god/dess or some other variation that combines masculine and feminine. The word "goddess" is derivative and diminutive in English, and we have rightly abandoned most of the "ess" forms—"poetess," "stewardess," "waitress," "authoress," "mistress" (feminine of "master"). I look forward to the day when we also abandon "actress" and "goddess." In some cases we have found new terms ("server," "flight attendant"); in other cases, we have made the masculine gender-neutral ("author," "poet"). Until we find a new term for "god," I prefer making the masculine gender-neutral and supporting that use with a variety of female and male names and images—as well as nonhuman images.

Thus, for instance, when I call on Bridget, I call on the God whom some of my ancestors may have worshiped and others may have tried to destroy. I call on the God who gave both wisdom and healing to those who sought her. I call on the God who was named anew—and still worshiped—as St. Bridget. The waters of her well healed people of the villages, and the eternal flame at her shrine was tended first by "pagan" women and later by Catholic sisters.

Invoking Bridget helps worshipers to rid themselves of the dominant Western stereotypes of the female and feminine as weak, passive, and dependent and yet, because she is woman, helps keep our understanding of God as incarnate, embodied, of the earth and our daily lives. Calling on Bridget opens us to the sacred power that flows through the women, as well as the men, gathered for worship. And I must admit that when I call on Bridget (or another female God), I do stand a bit taller, and I mutter to myself, "Yes!"

When I call on Artemis, I stand with the women in Philippi who worshiped her, carved holy art on the rocks outside the city, and probably brought her into the church by bringing baptism with them as they became Christian.[21] Calling on Artemis helps ground worshipers in the ambiguity and creativity of the early church in its relation to its culture. Invoking Artemis opens us to the creative power of care and nurture—and also the risk of dying—as women give birth.

When I call on YHWH, I call on the God of the Hebrews, in whose tradition I partially stand, since we separated after the first century C.E. I call on the God who, according to the traditions, led the Hebrews out of Egypt but did not lead Hagar out of the wilderness, who made the first earthlings (the two that have come to be called Adam and Eve) and told them to be vegetarians as well as not to eat the fruit of the tree of good and evil, and who commanded Amos to proclaim the necessity for justice in Israel's life if it was to be faithful to its God.

Using such a plurality of names, particularly the female ones, connects me as a woman with the powers of the universe in a way that—for me and for many, many other white women—traditional patriarchal images do not. It expands our imaginations and opens us to new inspirations and insights. It nurtures and empowers women and thus helps move us toward mutual relation *with other women* as well as with men. The diversity helps us to draw on and affirm the many interrelated heritages in which white Christian women and men stand, with both their resources and limitations.

Names, however, although they can be exciting and powerful, also have limitations. They inevitably image God as a being, like us, but more so. They thus tend to perpetuate hierarchical constructs of God. Human images should be complemented by those drawn from the natural world. God as the rock of my salvation is a traditional one. I sometimes image God as a Siamese cat, as I mentioned above.

Images like the Siamese cat are fine for personal meditation and worship. But congregational worship needs shared images that communicate dimensions of sacred power and open us to that power. The ocean can be a rich and powerful image, particularly for coastal people. It is a very real source of life to the globe; it is a source of inspiration and healing, of life and death. Its waters are like the waters of wombs—again life-giving (and female!). Its rhythms suggest eternity, yet at the same time it reminds us of our intrinsic connectedness with the earth. It is profoundly nondualistic.

There are many such powerful images. Congregations can experiment with finding those that are powerful to them. The important thing is to include images drawn from the nonhuman world.

Images of ultimacy and of inclusiveness are also important. For me, images that evoke these dimensions of God are those of lover and beloved, friend. God is lover of the universe; we are all beloveds of God—the grass, the sparrows, elite white men, us. God is beloved. "You have made us for yourself, and our hearts are restless until they find their rest in you."

"Friend" gathers up much of the feminist reflection and my own experience; it is a preeminently nonhierarchical image, preeminently suggestive of mutuality, shared power, openness, trust, and fidelity. It captures much of what is also suggested in parental images without the unequal power relationship. It suggests eros—attraction and longing and sexual energy—without absorption into the one loved. "Friend God" is spoken in power, love, and commitment. Acknowledging that God speaks "Friend Elly" is to receive power, love, and commitment. These are terms of endearment, delight, and trust; but to speak them involves taking a risk as well as falling in love.

I think such images evoke ultimacy and inclusiveness because they are all non-hierarchical. They are gender, racial, and species inclusive. They are nonmilitaristic. And although they include nurturing dimensions of power that "mother" also can suggest, they imply an equality of power and an intentional, freely chosen commitment and steadfastness.

For Christians, of course, Jesus is a powerful image of God, an image of grace, of abiding, of new creation. Over and over, Jesus spoke of God in terms of graciousness and commitment to those marginalized by the dominant culture: be merciful; forgive; invite the prodigal, the poor, and the outcast to the feast; tend to the man robbed on the highway; look for the lost coin and lost sheep; go the second mile; turn the other cheek. Be gracious and bring into your care or to your table those who are on the margins of society or who are your enemies.

Jesus' own life was consistent with this understanding of God. He ate with tax collectors and sinners. He brought those who had been outcast through physical or emotional trauma into his community. Although I see Jesus' own ministry primarily to those marginalized through economic hardship, ritual uncleanness, and disability, by extension his story points to a God who cares for all marginalized people and who is actively creating a new community in which they are full citizens.

However central he is for Christians, Jesus is a specific, particular image, or revelation, of God. He does not reveal a generic God or a generic humanity. He was a first-century Jewish male bearing witness to a Jewish culturally informed understanding and experience of God. As such, he is not the only or even the fullest revelation of God. Many people and other creatures reveal dimensions of the heart of the universe, the powers at work in the universe, to us. Nevertheless, for Christians, he was and continues to be a powerful revelation of the heart of the universe. Jesus' life affirms that the powers of the universe are consistent with the longings of human and other hearts for community and justice. It communicates that the powers of the universe are at work to bring satisfaction and healing to those hearts. It opens us to the outlines of a way of living that is possible, desirable, respectful, and abundant for all. It challenges and empowers us to move toward that vision personally, interpersonally, and socially.

As we experiment with images and names, I think that what is important is to use a plurality of images that continue to expand our understanding of God. Using both human and nonhuman images consistently helps us to deepen our understanding of God's concern for all of creation. Using a variety of images and acknowledging their sources, contexts, and limitations can help to communicate both the multifaceted nature of God and the understanding of God as ultimate and inclusive.

"You shall love the Sovereign your
God with all your heart, and with all
your soul, and with all your strength,
and with all your mind; and your
neighbor as yourself." "You shall love
the Sovereign your God with all your
heart, and with all your soul, and with
all your strength, and with all your
mind; and your neighbor as yourself."

4

ETHICS OF CREATION AND
NEW CREATION

The Spirit of the Lord is upon me,
  because he has anointed me
    to bring good news to the poor.
He has sent me to proclaim release to the captives
  and recovery of sight to the blind,
    to let the oppressed go free,
to proclaim the year of the Lord's favor.

               —*Luke 4:18–19*

God and the world belong together. God and the world *are* together. Dominant traditional theology speaks of God as being the creator of the universe in addition to being active in it. These doctrines of creation have typically been constructed in one of two ways. They have served as background, while in the foreground are the cross and salvation, the heart of the Christian message and experience. After all, how often do you hear someone testify to her/his experience of creation? And these doctrines have served as a basis for a general (and universal) morality, related to but also separate from a morality for Christians. I think of both the Lutheran law/gospel duality and the Catholic natural-law tradition. This function of the doctrine of creation also puts creation if not in the background, at least in a place of secondary importance to the heart of the Christian life.

Further, as we all know by now, the dominant church has had difficulty in affirming creation even in the background or in a place of secondary importance. Traditional Christian theology has been anti-body and anti–natural world and has legislated an ethic of suspicion and control of the body and the natural world.

Recent interest in ecological justice, feminist analyses of the connections among "woman," "body," and "nature," and earth-based spirituality movements have led to a renewed examination and to new constructions of the doctrine of creation. In this chapter I continue the work of new construction, from a white feminist perspective.

I will do so under five rubrics: historical-social constructions of creation; toward a new (white, feminist) construction of creation; creation is new creation; creation and sin; and struggle and transformation.

HISTORICAL-SOCIAL CONSTRUCTIONS OF "NATURE," "WOMAN," AND "MAN"

A feminist construction recognizes that creation, which includes the natural world and human beings, exists in complex multiple, overlapping, contradictory locations and histories. "Woman" does not have a universal meaning in this country; neither do "nature" and "man."

For African American women and men, those terms have been constructed by white elites and imposed on blacks to maintain control and to justify that control. The meanings of these terms reflect actual legal, social, and economic conditions and a host of images and stereotypes.

The contexts and conditions of most African Americans during slavery were, of course, bondage and with it a construction of blackness that was subhuman, less than human, certainly less than adult human. "Woman" and "man," therefore, were really not relevant terms as whites saw black people. Blacks were property, they were animals—beasts of burden—and they were "boy," "servant," "sex object." Black women were viewed as breeders, much the same as cows and pigs. Records from slave auctions testify over and over that slaves were described and evaluated in terms of their capacity to be like farm animals, producing livelihood and profit for their owners.[1]

Many black slaves and tenant farmers lived with and worked the land within the context of racism. I wonder to what extent that connection, in the eyes of the white dominant culture, has led to the equation of "dirt" (brown and black) with "bad"—dirty jokes, being dirty, soiling one's clothes. I well remember the looks and remarks of my mother when I came into the house with dirt on my clothes. They were never positive, much less cognizant of dirt as created by God; instead, I was told to "clean up!"

The bodies of black women don't generally look like the norm—Miss America, movie stars, the women in commercials. But in addition to shape and size, black women's bodies range in color from light-coffee to ebony and generally exhibit other distinctive racial features. Yet still today, when a few, token black women do appear in the normative categories above, they are light-skinned and look much like their white women counterparts.

Further, daily brutal pain and suffering were inflicted on their body-spirits. Embodiedness was agony, not only because of physical abuse, which was horrible enough, but also because of a lack of sanctioned possibility for spiritual and creative expression. Alice Walker wrote of many who "forced their minds to desert their bodies" and "were driven to a numb and bleeding madness by the springs of creativity in them for which there was no release."[2]

After slavery, in urban areas black men competed with waves of European (white) immigrant men and women for jobs in the mills and factories of the North; they competed and typically lost out. The jobs open to black women were often as domestic workers—nannies and housecleaners. The so-called nurturing and caring roles were imposed on them. Further, black women were expected to care for *whites,* who were, in a very real sense, their structural enemies.

A white construction of the natural world was also imposed on enslaved African Americans. Much of this world was a place of bondage for African Americans. The fields and plantations on which they worked were sites of pain and suffering, both from nature itself and from white overseers and masters. Enslaved people lived in relation to the rhythms of nature, but the relation was one of ceaseless labor and constant exposure to heat, cold, rain, and sleet.

The natural world was also a site of bitter paradox. Women and men working in the fields gained competence and knowledge, but they received no acknowledgment of or return for their skill. They remained beasts—and their owners received social status and economic power.

At the same time, however, African Americans created their own constructions in response to these conditions, images, and stereotypes. Those constructions are multiple and complex and are difficult for a white woman to begin to identify. Nevertheless . . .

Slave women and men worked the land; they knew it intimately and well. They knew its rhythms and resources—its medicinal properties and its bounty as well as its profit to the owner. Margaret Walker movingly explores a positive legacy of that experience as Vryey and Innes Brown sought to establish themselves as farmers on land promised them by the government after the Civil War.[3] But the Browns knew, intimately and well, that even after legal freedom, their access to land was precarious at best and dependent on the will of the KKK and/or local white farmers and town citizens. They also knew that the land available to them was the poorest, the most often flooded out, or later the most polluted. Nevertheless land, however limited after slavery, meant a measure of freedom and a space of competence and power.

This legacy has continued. According to Edward J. Pennick, since the times of slavery, landownership has been recognized as central to gaining economic independence, and "the desire of land led blacks to acquire nearly fifteen million acres by 1920."[4]

Most southern blacks, however, went from slavery to sharecropping, and that heritage created an even more contradictory relation to the land. The autobiography of Nate Shaw, an Alabama sharecropper, reflects this construction.[5] Shaw made the land that he farmed prosper, but the structural relationships between blacks and whites in

Alabama during much of his lifetime kept him indebted to and dependent on white farmers, bankers, and businesspeople. His story reveals again and again his intimate and sophisticated knowledge and his ability to make a living from his labor. Land was his sustenance; it was his life. At the same time, it and the sources of the necessary materials and capital belonged to others. For many of his neighbors, this reality meant insecurity, dependence, caution, deference, and obedience toward whites.

This created a multiple and profound complexity. The dominant economic and cultural ethos stated: (1) the land should be worked; (2) if you worked the land (and worked hard), you would "improve" the land—give it value and "civilize" it; (3) you not only could survive but also could make a profit; (4) success was a sign of God's favor; and (5) if you remained poor, you were lazy, sinful, no-good. Sharecroppers worked the land, working very hard, and barely survived. Certainly they improved and cultivated the land, and thus civilized it, changing it from a part of "wilderness" to "civilization," but that did not "elevate" them from animal to human being.[6] Making a profit was outside the realm of reality, although black farmers knew (at least many did) that Jesus was with them in their poverty. So land inevitably had to be viewed in practical and utilitarian ways that supported capitalism; but it also remained distant, a major part of the insecurity and alienation of their lives and complicit, as it were, in a system of oppression.

Still today, even ownership is no guarantee of security. Black farmers are in the most precarious position of all farmers, losing their land at ten times the rate of white farmers.[7] Between 1982 and 1987, nearly one-third of black farmers went out of business.[8]

It was inevitable, given this legacy, that urban space would be seen as offering more freedom than the natural world, the land. Blacks migrated by the thousands to work in the factories. I expect that many fled to the urban North not only to get jobs but also to escape land that was unreliable, land that demanded incredibly hard work with little promise of any return, land that consisted of broiling sun, drenching rain, numbing cold, and unrelenting insects. But once again, blacks encountered the racist construction of reality. They were domestics; they competed with newly arriving European immigrants for jobs—and generally lost.

Further, both the land and the urban spaces inhabited by African Americans were and are among the worst polluted and most dangerous to human health in the country. Emilie Townes has bluntly written that toxic-waste landfills are the current forms of lynching.[9] She notes, for instance, that three of the four hazardous-waste landfills in the South are located where the majority of people are black, and she adds, "The nation's largest hazardous waste landfill is in predominantly Black and poor Sumter County in Alabama." Similarly, there are ninety-four "uncontrolled toxic waste sites in Atlanta" in the areas where just under 83 percent of the black population lives![10]

Noncultivated land has played a somewhat different but also complex role in African American experience. In an exploration of the wilderness theme in black women's heritage, Delores Williams finds that before the Civil War, land outside of the plantations meant freedom, escape, and a place where the slave could meet God. The slave narratives speak often of individuals "going into the woods to pray." Slaves typically met for worship in the forest or by the river, in secret and away from white eyes. After the war, however, wilderness was a part of the insecurity of the lives of southern blacks and typically played no role in creating security.[11]

A white person could conclude from this history that African Americans have been largely alienated from the natural world, given the racist construction of "nature," "man," and "woman." And yet I don't think this is the whole story. Nate Shaw's case, for instance, suggests a more complex relation. For him, in contrast to his neighbors, land was certainly to be worked, but it also seemed to be a context and a condition of freedom, power, and the exercise of competence. Apparently he did not see himself like the land, dependent on others, especially white monied men. Rather, he seemed to see himself, at least to some extent, in charge of the land he farmed. In growing cotton and corn, in raising vegetables and harvesting fruit from the trees on his land, he had both freedom and power. He was proud of what he accomplished and knew that he was good. Further, although the land seemed to have had more economic value to Shaw than aesthetic or spiritual value, more utilitarian value than intrinsic, it was not simply a resource. The land was not to be used up, worn out, or seen only as a source for profit.

Given the realities of sharecropping, it would have been impossible for Shaw to make a personal profit from the land, but I do not think that this was simply a situation imposed on him by the economic structure of sharecropping. My sense is that he experienced and understood a more interdependent relationship with the land. Land was the source of survival and sufficiency, but it was not to be destroyed. One took what was needed and what allowed one to prosper in the teeth of every effort to prevent that—including, in Shaw's case, twelve years in prison for challenging a deputy sheriff's attempt to attach a neighbor's animals, equipment, and land after both had joined a sharecroppers' union. Beyond that, one left the land to renew itself. Neither Shaw's actions nor his speech in any way reflected Francis Bacon's construction of nature as being "in bondage" to "man."

I see this interdependent relationship implicitly in terms of the land. It is more explicit as Shaw talked about the farm animals. He spoke of caring for them as one cares for his family, of keeping them "fat and pretty," of feeding them three times a day. He stated, "Just like I et—them animals, my mules or my horses, I considered the next thing to my family."[12]

Another example of the complexity of the constructions of the relationships between specific groups of people and the natural world comes from Robert Coles's interviews, in *Children of Crisis,* with children and parents of migrant, sharecropping, and mountain families. Many of these families were white, so the social location is different in terms of race, but there are enough parallels to shed some further light on realities and constructions of "woman," "man," and "nature" by very marginalized groups in this country.

In those interviews, people affirmed that the land belonged to God—but also to the stranger—the boss. In no case did it belong to them. Yet the land revealed a power other than that of the boss: "When a sharecropper boy draws a home, it is small and inconsequential in appearance, a mere spot on the thick, powerful earth."[13] Further, although life on the land was problematic and tenuous, the earth and the seasons offered consistency and knowledge and a space for competence. "Sharecropper children view the fields and the crops as life's one reliable element."[14] As one parent said, "At least we have the fields."[15] Another noted with pride, "The kids come in and tell me that the first leaf has turned, and we'll be having cooler weather . . . [or] that the water is beginning to run low . . . [or] that we forgot to spray a corner of the land."[16] Coles concludes that the persistent question for these families is whether to stay or leave. The land in a sense is a source of misery, but the families he was in contact with would miss it; their lives were strongly tied to the rhythms of planting, growing, and harvesting. So the land might be both fickle and reliable, a source of both insecurity and security; in bondage to owners other than themselves, the land was also powerful.

This sense of the natural world operating independently and powerfully apart from people is also a theme in the literature of Toni Morrison. Barbara Christian points out that fire, air, and water are powerful, independent, and indeed spiritual forces at work in Morrison's novels and also that they, like her characters, are affected by patterns of oppression.[17] The natural world is constructed in light of social realities; it also operates independently and, as it were, imposes its own construction on the people within it.

There is another critically important response to the natural world, a response described by Alice Walker: the creation of beauty out of nature. Black women created beauty; they created it in gardens and flowerpots, as well as in quilts and other items they made for daily use. Walker wrote of her mother: "Only when my mother is working in her flowers . . . she is radiant. . . . She is involved in work her soul must have. Ordering the universe in the image of her personal conception of Beauty."[18] Beauty may not have been intrinsic to nature—at least that is not a major theme—but it is a possibility. Nature might be ambiguous about its ability to feed the body, but with the creative activity of people, it could feed the spirit.

Finally, womanists have been engaged in major reconstructions of "woman," "nature," and "man," particularly the first two. They have been reclaiming blackness, their embodiedness as beautiful and precious, as gifts to cherish. Baby Sugg's sermon in Morrison's *Beloved* is an incredibly powerful and beautiful testimony to this renaming:

> Here in this here place, we flesh; flesh that weeps, laughs; flesh that dances on bare feet in grass. Love it. Love it hard. Yonder they do not love your flesh. They despise it. . . . No more do they love the skin on your back. Yonder they flay it. And O my people they do not love your hands. Those they only use, tie, bind, chop off and leave empty. Love your hands! Love them. Raise them up and kiss them. Touch others with them, pat them together, stroke them on your face 'cause they don't love that either. *You* got to love it, *you!*[19]

In her writings, Alice Walker has also identified themes that suggest an embodied spiritual connection between people and the natural world. In *The Color Purple,* Shug talks about her spiritual journey toward a God known in sexual pleasure and a mystical oneness with trees that is both ecstatic and painful. Similarly, in her essay "Am I Blue?," Walker movingly writes of communication between herself and a horse, but as with trees, Walker emphasizes a connection in the experience of violence, the violence that some humans do to animals just as they do to other humans—specifically, the violence done to a horse and the violence done to slaves.[20] In both of these writings, the communication between a black woman and "nature" (a tree, a horse) is shaped by a specific history and ecosocial location that, even in its potential mysticism, experiences a shared pain.

In African American history, then, at least on this continent, the legacy and meanings of "woman" include "mule of the world"—breeder, worker, totally vulnerable to white men, ugly, unclean, of no intrinsic worth, but also resister, survivor, Angela Davis as well as Aunt Jemima, Shug as well as Celie, profoundly lovable and beloved.

Similarly, "nature" is wilderness, power, the possession of oppressors, a place of toil, the shared recipient of violence and bondage, a precarious resource for economic independence, and perhaps for some, a place of power, freedom, and competence.

And "man" is animal, possession as land is possession, dependent as animals and earth are dependent, but also worker, provider, owner, skilled resource person and administrator.

A thorough study of these constructions would draw on much more literature and examine more closely the changes over time and the relationships between women and men, not just the relationships with the natural world—and not just with the land and farm animals. In New England, for instance, African American men were sailors; after the Civil War, African American men were cowboys. One would have to examine a whole range of relationships and constructions. My point here is simply to point to the complexity and differences in constructions as they have been shaped by interwoven realities of racism, patriarchy, and classism in this country.

White, or European American, feminists, primarily ecofeminists, have explored in detail the meanings of "woman" and "nature." As a result of this analysis, ecofeminists have highlighted for other feminists and for nonfeminist environmental activists and theoreticians the necessity of connecting patriarchal and class oppression with the destruction of the earth. At the same time, I see in some of their writings unexamined assumptions that reflect relatively privileged social locations, assumptions that result in collusion with oppression.

For instance, the editor of *Sisters of the Earth,* an anthology of writings by women about women and the earth, dedicates the book "To Gaia—fertile mother, wise sister" and then quotes Susan Griffin: "This earth is my sister; / I love her daily grace, her silent daring, and how loved I am."[21] The dedication and the selection from Griffin, when read in context, reflect several ways in which ecofeminism sometimes reflects unexamined and thus oppressive privilege. First, although Griffin speaks of the earth as her sister, the assumption is that she is speaking for all women, not just herself as an individual. The title of the book from which the quotation is taken is *Woman and Nature: The Roaring Inside Her.* Women are family with the rest of nature. In part that means that women share some common experiences with the rest of the natural world—impoverishment, abuse, rape. But the kinship goes beyond that: we are *naturally,* biologically and ontologically, family, and a major expression of that kinship is our capacity to be nurturing, generous, graceful, and also wild—spontaneous, vital, fecund. Further, that kinship is spiritual, not simply physiological, and we can experience it as oneness with nature and thus with all that is.

> We are women. We rise from the wave. We are gazelle and doe, . . . we are air, we are flame. . . . We are woman and nature. And he says he cannot hear us speak.
> But we hear.[22]

The problems with those assertions are or should be obvious. Both "woman" and "nature" have some kind of ahistorical essence that can be known. Both uncritically reflect very white, middle-class, idealized constructs about women and nature. They make sense for and have tremendous appeal to many white middle-class women whose lives have been socially constricted and sheltered and who long for more freedom but not chaos or violence, who seek freedom and safety at the same time.

Further, as I wrote above, somehow we can know this essence—of woman and nature uncorrupted, this ahistorical reality, this ontology. We can transcend our social constructs or, rather, decide that *our* constructs are real whereas others' are the result of social realities that can and should be changed.

Finally, though Griffin does try to overcome the dualism of body-soul and nature-culture, she almost eliminates culture. Women are alienated from nature as a result of patriarchal culture. But she does not then suggest that reconciliation may come through a different cultural construction. Rather she locates spirit in nature, assumes a *natural* harmony, or kinship, between the two and tends to equate spirit with biological processes. There is thus little room left for the exercise of mind and the development of culture, which, in her use of the word, is not *natural.* I write "almost" and "tends" because she uses words—very powerfully—and words are culture.

Is "man," then, "patriarchy," "culture," "bad," by nature unable to connect with the nurturing and wildness of the natural world? What about men of color and very poor white men who participate very tenuously in patriarchal institutional structures of power and privilege? Are those men, and those who do participate and shape culture, of a different nature from the rest of us?

Certainly not all ecofeminists would agree with the positions I am ascribing to Griffin in *Woman and Nature.* Certainly ecofeminists are activists for social justice and continue to hold before the rest of us the need to connect ecological and social issues. But I do find themes of romantic vitalism and unexamined, unearned white privilege in some ecofeminist literature. For women and men whose heritage is body, nature, and who know the natural and social world to be hard, oppressive, and ambiguous, that kinship, to the extent that there is one, will also be much more ambiguous. Activism to create a just society, a new culture, becomes much more important than a celebration of kinship with nature. If instead of making such questionable generalizations, we begin with our own diversity of stories and histories, as well as listen to those of women whose realities are quite different from our own, and if we recognize that all of our realities are shaped by structures of oppression and ecosocial location, then we can begin to create (as well as respond to) new constructions of "woman," "nature," and "man."

For instance, a non-working-class white woman's history may also have been tied to slavery, but as part of the owning class, she had a legacy of learning how to become a lady, a complex designation that included graciousness and feminine charm on the one hand and managerial skills on the other. She was expected to be endlessly nurturing and reconciling, tactful and pleasing to others. She was innocent—pure, living in a sheltered world—and in a sense above sexuality. An acquaintance of mine, whose social location and history is one of identifying "woman" with "lady," observes that she learned to equate sexuality with genitals and to save it for her husband, thus distancing herself from her sexuality.[23] In contrast, as breeders and animals, black women were sexual (and expected to be "loose" and available to white men).

Legally, economically, and politically, both black and white women were powerless, but the white woman had social status and, within the household, power over the black woman. Both women were the prey of white men; within the household, the white woman could also abuse the black woman. Both women were victims, but the black woman had access to a community of resistance generally not available to the white woman. To a significant extent, the black woman's church challenged the dominant legacy; to a significant extent, the white woman's church justified the dominant legacies—about her and her treatment of black women.

White women were also expected to nurture, but with an important difference. For the white woman, nurture supposedly reflected her (our) nature. For the black woman, however, for whom "woman" did not equal "feminine," nurture did not make her any more human in the eyes of whites. White women were also expected to care for white men, who—again as with black women—were often their enemies, but white women had no separate subculture by which to name their fathers, husbands, brothers, and uncles as the "enemy."

For a white woman in the above social context and history, "nature" also meant something largely different from what it meant to a black woman. The white woman (lady) was surrounded by a cultivated, domesticated nature that provided her with sustenance and beauty. Nature, the natural world, was nurturing for body and spirit for the white woman, and she probably participated in the ongoing creation of sustenance and beauty as she tended her yard and gardens, even though she had gardeners and yardmen to work there also. Such a location carried security, pride, and a sense of ownership, although her husband was actually financially responsible for the house and grounds. The black and the white women both sought beauty, both made beauty in nature, but the gestalt of even that experience makes the one quite different from the other.

Williams has written that before the Civil War, slaves saw wilderness as escape and a place for meeting God. To what extent did the white lady see uncivilized nature as freedom? To what extent did she feel like the bonsai tree—shaped, cultivated, and diminished by the structures in which she lived? She might well have watched the trees bend in a hurricane and felt the stirrings of a roaring inside her. Or did the security, the responsibilities, the unrelieved messages of what it meant to be a "woman" (i.e., "lady") drown out any questions, any doubts, any restlessness? If she was competent at what she did, perhaps her self-esteem did not suffer. If she was abused by her husband, did she question those messages then? Did she draw any parallels between the natural world and her own situation? Did nature ever come to mean freedom or escape, as it did to slaves? Did she ever see nature and herself connected in a different kind of bondage from the slave woman's or in different but also similar kinds of bondage?

In my case, I grew up in a small town near the Atlantic Ocean. I rode my bike all over the area and spent summers at the ocean, where my sister and I created endless stories on the beach. Swimming, walking for miles on the sand, and biking meant freedom for me, freedom from expectations that made me feel I was never good enough, freedom to be and to imagine and to dream. So the natural world offered space for positive human activity and identity. And as I pursued these activities, the rhythms of ocean and sky—the colors, sounds, and smells of earth, pine trees, sand, water, and air—seeped into my being and became a part of me.

I rejoice in this heritage, but I am also deeply aware that the opportunity to spend so much of my life at the ocean was denied, in different ways, to white children whose families could not afford time at the ocean or who did not live near it and to children of color. Since my parents owned a succession of cottages at the ocean, I could stay there all summer. The beach, in southern Delaware, was off-limits to blacks. There were no signs, but everyone understood the boundaries. Nor did I bike, except very occasionally, into the area of town where African Americans lived, though I was free to bike everywhere else. I don't recall ever being told, but I knew that the world—at least what I could reach on my bike—was mine, except for a small segregated area that was vaguely threatening. I was, in this respect, a good white girl-child.

The historical-social locations of black women and of middle-class white women reflect significantly different constructions of "woman" and "nature," as well as some commonalities. If I were to explore women in other locations or to refine these further, still more constructions would emerge, sharing in and responding to dominant cultural values and beliefs and enabling people to survive in interlocking social structures. And even within those many locations, individuals respond differently. We are not simply carbon copies of our social locations; we are actors, seeking to survive and to live lives of meaning and value, often with great courage and pain.

TOWARD A NEW (WHITE, FEMINIST) CONSTRUCTION OF CREATION

A white feminist post-Christendom construction of creation is a construction of humanity and the natural world in light of the theological affirmation that women, men, and the natural world are related to God and one another, as creatures of God and one another and as creative agents themselves. It includes, therefore, a new construction of "woman," "man," and "nature" within this larger context, an ultimately universally inclusive set of relationships. It means that I must speak concretely and relatively and yet make universal statements about "humanity" as I dared to make about "God." So, the following is my contribution to, not a position on or a finished reconceptualization of, a feminist construction of creation.

CONSTRUCTION AND RESPONSE

My construction of creation begins with the affirmation that creation is ongoing. It is not a finished activity of God serving as a backdrop to more important, redeem-

ing actions. In the relational theology I have been using, to speak of God as creator
is to speak of a creative and ever-flowing power throughout the universe. Wherever
God is, creation occurs. To paraphrase Mary Daly, creation is a verb, creating, bringing forth life—new life, change, growth, decay, death, life. There is an ongoing seasonal rhythm of birth, growth, decay, death, dormancy, life. There are ongoing
complex processes and relationships within humanity and perhaps other creatures of
not only physical but also psychical and spiritual birth, growth, death, and new life.
Within the human realm, there are new dreams, visions, inventions, discoveries in
art, reflections, politics, and the actions of making things. The world is alive and
always in motion. When I talk about creation, I am not talking about once upon a
time, in the beginning, but now.

This construction of creation questions the traditional emphasis on structure,
from which a natural law is derived. It questions a construction of the universe in
which structure and rationality have priority over process and change, over conflict
and even chaos, and over actions emerging from threats, dreams, values, fears, and
eros. It questions the assumptions of the construction that socially located individuals have the transcendent capacity to know the rational and universal structure of
the universe. It questions preeminently the assumptions that the universe has a
rational, moral structure and that socially located individuals can know and legislate
that morality for all.

Questioning a universal moral structure knowable primarily to white Western
men and—more recently—to many of us white feminists, however, does not lead
me to deny whether any knowledge of the universe is possible. We do construct reality, but a relational construction intrinsically affirms *responding* as well as constructing. And in responding, we come to know both structure and change.

The constructions themselves are a result of at least three threads of our relationality: (1) responses to "cues," "voices," what we see and hear; (2) history-her-
itage; and (3) particular interests and concerns of those in power (i.e., those in a
position to construct). We see and feel changes in the weather, and we construct
myths, meanings, and shelters relative to our experiences. We don't simply make up
meaning and institutions arbitrarily. To emphasize human reality as a constructed
reality is not to fall into a form of solipsism. It does not mean that we can't know
others and the natural world. Our constructions arise out of our interactions with
others and the natural world.

The relationship between construction and response is itself complex, and our
constructions can become so powerful that they shut us off from further or alternative cues of relationships to which we might respond. Much of our response to our
past is response to an already constructed past. We inherit meanings, myths, and
shelter patterns and continue to interpret the weather in light of that heritage.
Further, since Western social construction is particularly related to those in posi-

tions of power, many people in the United States rely on scientists—meteorologists—on the evening television for their understanding of the weather, although some may still depend on other sources, such as aching bones, the alignment of planets, or a myth about human relationships with the earth.

The power and right of certain groups of people to construct reality for the rest of us is extremely difficult to question. This is particularly true of certain scientific constructions that simply are assumed to be true, that is, assumed somehow to be a correct understanding of what is really happening. These two factors—our past and the interests-perspectives of those in positions of social power—mean that our attentiveness to cues, our responsiveness to others, is highly selective and that our understanding of those cues is prejudged. For instance, I recently read the following statement from a scientist: "Down the centuries and throughout the world people have believed that they can control supernatural powers by following magic rituals."[24] The use of such words as "control" and "magic" reflects a modern, Western scientific effort to interpret the past. If we accept such interpretations, it is difficult not to believe that a scientific-based culture is superior to such a "primitive" one, and thus do supposedly descriptive statements support racism. It is also difficult to be responsive to dimensions within that past that might cue us into other interpretations. Scientific interpretations too often have the effect of distancing us from the past so that we don't consider imaginatively entering into the situation or trying to draw any parallels with or similarities to our own experiences. The ritual might be one of preparation rather than control, as when an athlete performs rituals of preparation. It might be a ritual of communion, such as communication with the buffalo, just as we have rituals of communion that we call holy. Further, if the author had been open to other aspects, to the context of the ritual, he might have pondered the role of community in indigenous cultures or looked at other features of indigenous life and asked whether control was really that important. It just might be that control is much more important in this culture than in the culture he is writing about. But given the hierarchical patterns within which the author lives, it was probably close to inevitable that he responded as he did.

Another, everyday example can be seen in homophobic responses to people's actions. Within the prevailing homophobia of the dominant culture, a middle-class man shaped by that culture will see very little of two other men walking down the street. He may see only that they are holding hands and ignore all the clues that point to their love and care for each other, their happiness, their middle-class or professional dress, cues that might otherwise tend to make them acceptable and harmless to the viewer. Although these two features of our lives—relationality and social construction—are dynamic and themselves relational, the strength of social construction for blocking openness to cues, to voices, can be and often is, at least in the short run, dominating.

This pattern characterizes interpretations of the natural world as well as the social one. Shaped by a Victorian society that was patriarchal, racist, and violent, Darwin saw conflict, the struggle to survive, the predation of the strong on the weak, and mindless "natural" selection. He responded to certain cues that reflected his culture rather than to others, to examples of cooperation, for instance, or to instances of what Annie Dillard called "beauty and grace."[25]

Responses to others in a racist, classist, and patriarchal culture similarly block many cues we might otherwise be open to. We see, feel, and know what we have been constructed to see, feel, and know. The social constructions of "woman" and "nature" dramatically inhibit our capacity to respond in ways that do not continue to oppress one another and the natural world.

Nevertheless, the constructions themselves emerged out of a combination of response and construction, *and* we are capable of different kinds of responses. We do not have to accept the scientific interpretation of indigenous ritual, or the homophobic interpretation of the two men, or the racist, sexist constructions of women and the natural world. We are capable of making different responses and constructions both because we have alternative constructions available and because we have within us the capacity to be open to—to see—other dimensions of our relatives, those with whom we are related, ultimately the universe. Thus, feminists and some scientists, for instance, are reinterpreting dimensions of the natural world through a new complex configuration of a somewhat different social construction, using methodologies of and responses to both traditional and new cues. Some of these point to the existence of cooperation in the natural world. The sugar maple, for instance, pulls water up from deep within the earth, reaching deeper than surrounding plants can reach, and then "shares" the excess with them.[26] Biologist Lynn Margulis hypothesizes that cooperation in the natural world is more basic than conflict.[27] Others point out that animals generally do not dominate one another, the stereotype of the lion as "king" of the jungle notwithstanding. As Murray Bookchin has written: "Put simply, animals do not 'dominate' each other in the same way that a human elite dominates, and often exploits, an oppressed social group. Nor do they 'rule' through institutional forms of systematic violence."[28] Both Disney and Darwin have a lot to answer for.

Put theologically, revelation is ongoing and basic. If indeed we are relational beings, if a relational theology is not *only* another construction, revelation is intrinsic to the universe. Actually, both "communication" and "revelation" are basic. The latter is a making known of what has been hidden, and certainly much has been hidden, given the character of modern Western constructions. But ultimately, at least dimensions of the universe are knowable; communication is possible, and subjects are expressing themselves to subjects.

As I have written above, I think that much more communication and transformation than we have yet experienced is possible. We are not only relations, shaped by and shaping others; we can honor, explore, and enjoy—as well as challenge and defend—one another across a wide range of species. We can be *open* to one another.

Some constructions facilitate that openness more than others do. The construction I am developing in this book has that intention and, I hope, that effect. One of my reasons for not giving up on the church is that for all its faults, the theological constructions it has developed contain the mandate to do justice in a way that facilitates this openness. Churches, synagogues, temples, and now mosques in this country are still the only enduring organizations that do have that mandate.

Further, as I said above, constructions are not totally arbitrary. Spiraling in and through all our many relationships is the longing for, the yearning for, "at-homeness," belonging somewhere. We want to be loved and accepted by another or others; we want to belong someplace. And this connection, this positive relationship, has intrinsic meaning and value. We also yearn not only to survive but to live in beauty and wholeness. And when life is denied, we will fight. Further, this capacity within us enables us to enter imaginatively into the lives of others—to grasp their pain and joy—both to know it when it is named and, at least to some extent, to share it, that is, to stand with those experiencing it.

We have what I call "heart." Pascal was right: the heart has reasons reason doesn't know. "Heart" is an image, a metaphor for a gestalt of feeling, mind, imagination, and experience. It seeks to name this capacity to respond from a depth of being-in-relation. It is, as it were, a reservoir of our connectedness, our embeddedness, in the spirit-nature of the universe. It is my heart speaking when I ache for being at home in the universe, for the presence of God. It is my heart speaking when I experience despair. It is my heart speaking when I am transformed by seeing the elderly black woman plod wearily to the back of the bus. Our hearts can be touched; we can be moved; we can be converted. Our hearts need constructions appropriate for sustained commitment to justice for all; otherwise we might respond to individual cases but fail to relate a specific situation to a larger systemic reality. But without our hearts, we would simply be imprisoned in whatever dominant construction exists.

We are capable of responding in this way—from our hearts. But that remains one response among others, one openness to certain cues among others. So social construction is not only a reality but also a necessity. I want and need a social construction that reflects the values of heart, that pushes and enables us to look at ourselves and the natural world in terms of justice, sustainability, and well-being. A feminist theological construction of humanity and the natural world can help provide that framework. The rest of this chapter is an initial effort to construct a such a world.

HUMAN AND OTHER CREATURES

From my Christian feminist perspective, I affirm that our hearts long for what we call God as well as for specific others, for a relatedness to the universe, for being-at-home in the universe. I also affirm that we can and do experience that relatedness. The testimony of saints and seers and of mystics and worshipers the world over witnesses to the reality of that kind of relationship.

Further, oppression, violence stemming from social systems and cultural beliefs and values, ugliness, and diseased contexts affront and shock our hearts. We *naturally* try to defend ourselves from these insults or to overcome them—that is, our hearts urge us to survive, resist, and live.

I think that for me, this is what it means to be made in the image of God—our hearts' responsiveness. But I extend that image to other creatures, who also have hearts. I simply do not know whether all creatures have hearts, but certainly many do. Ultimately, of course, the question of who images God and in what respect is not important. Western theologians have made much too much of that phrase in Genesis about being created in the image of God. What is important is that we must learn to live in God's world with respect, mutuality, joy, and abundance.

Out of the experience of our hearts and many different justice-centered theological constructions, I affirm certain principles that are actually similar to natural-law principles. But I do not know whether they have always been a part of creation. I don't know that they are laws written into the universe. I am convinced that they are true and necessary now. Among others, these are the principles of justice, wholeness, and creativity. Justice is necessary for life to flourish, and it is written on our hearts. We do not have to be Christian or Jewish to know that. Similarly, we yearn for well-being within and without. Personally, we long to live well, exercising our interests and talents, enjoying one another, creating new things and beings, creating and living in beauty. Interpersonally, we long for positive connection, for loving and being loved, for rootedness, for relation with the powers of justice and healing that ultimately connect us with the entire universe. And the principle of creativity affirms both that change is ongoing in creation *and* that it should be guided. Humanity is not a blot on creation; humanity is a part of creation at this time, and we have a responsibility to use our hearts and our minds to continue to shape change toward justice and wholeness. Put theologically, we are called to witness to new creation.

Understanding ourselves and others as created means for me that we are kin, not created object. Human beings, bugs, palm trees, and whales are not the art forms or objects fashioned by a creator but are family, kin. We are relatives of power(s) streaming through the universe, powers that include artistic creativity, as I described in the previous chapter, but as I also wrote, we share in those powers; we are not simply or primarily their result.

To speak of creaturehood with the image of kin is to bring me back to the relational theological framework I described earlier, this time to emphasize the relatedness among humanity, the natural world, and God. Indeed, to say that we are relational is to say that we are ecological beings. We cannot live without the contexts and conditions of our lives. For example, the very makeup of our bodies connects us to land and air; we cannot live in the ocean without either providing for the conditions we need for existence or undergoing significant adaptation.

Our ecological existence is not only physical and biological but also social. We become only in relationships, and whom and what we become is profoundly dependent on the quality and variety of relationships within which we exist. Human females living in patriarchal institutions become significantly different women from those living in nonpatriarchal societies. In a patriarchal and racist society, women of color become different women from white women. Children are profoundly shaped by abusive relationships in their families.

We live as part of larger ecological wholes. In light of my commitment to justice, life understood ecologically means that we must rename how humanity is similar to and different from other creatures. Traditionally, dominant theology has held that humanity is singular and essential and that it is not only distinct—in its capacity to reason (which actually meant European males)—but also superior. Humanity alone is made in the image of God, and Genesis at least affirmed that women as well as men were made in the image of God, a construction that European theologians denied to white women and many other women and men.

My construction is different from this traditional one. I believe that each species and each individual being has its own distinctiveness. The human species, individuals, and the different social groups—each of these has its own distinctiveness. However, I disagree that human distinctiveness lies in rationality and that we should consider ourselves superior in any fashion to other creatures. As groups, we are distinctive in the kinds of cultures and experiences we bring to the whole. As individuals, we are distinctive in our dreams, skills, and journeys. As a species, we are distinctive in our capacity to change ourselves and our ecosystems quickly and drastically. Our decisions can have far-reaching impact, much more far-reaching than the impact of decisions that any other species might make.[29] We can dream and plan and translate those visions and goals into action, with tremendous consequences. Other creatures may dream and envision, they may hope and plan and suffer and seek relief or improvement of their conditions, but the impact of their choices is limited.

If we are distinctive in many ways, so are other creatures. Rocks and ants and beaver have their own distinctivenesses, individually, as groups and as species. As within the human species, being different does not equal being better or worse or viewing those who are different from "us" as objects. The richness of our creatureliness is such that we can appreciate, respect, come to know, and even love others across the whole range of creaturehood. I think Buber was correct: an *I-thou* relation with a tree is possible. Insofar as I can know it, I think I have such a relationship with the three cats that share our household. I anticipate a time when we are much more aware of interspecies communication than we are now.

We are distinctive. We are also similar—although not the same. As with differences within the human species, so it is with differences among them. Our gestalts are not the same. Nevertheless, we have much in common. Within the human species, we share similar emotions: we feel pain, we experience ecstasy, we make commitments, we seek revenge or forgiveness. We all have the capacity to be part of nourishing, fulfilling relationships, of destructive ones, or of combinations of both. As I described above, we all have something I call "heart." I think that emphasizing reason is elitist not only toward the rest of creation but also within humanity. Not everyone has that capacity—at least, not everyone has equally well-developed reason—but each person is still a human being. But without heart and, with it, the desire to communicate, a person may no longer be human. My experience, which I acknowledge is limited, is that even people labeled as profoundly retarded have and reveal their hearts. When my mother was in a coma for the five days before she died, she still communicated at times with us. Her heart, physically and spiritually, continued to beat frail wings.

Because we have hearts, we experience grief and anger and love; we know the loss of someone important to us; we yearn to be loved and accepted and cherished; we yearn to be at home, to be connected with the others, with the universe. At our center, deep inside, we know what we need for a meaningful life. That is what we share, regardless of history, culture, power, and privilege. And it is a critical resource. Within and in addition to the ongoing struggle for justice, if we can also begin to meet one another at our centers, we will revolutionize and accelerate that struggle toward ecosystems that deeply value and facilitate mutuality. I don't know that "all real life is meeting," but a profound dimension of life is meeting.[30]

There are still other commonalities of being human. We all have cultures, languages, and ways of organizing our lives, although the content of those vary tremendously and the skills and interests of individuals in shaping (and the opportunities to shape) those patterns vary tremendously. In our difference is our commonality, so to speak.

Some of this human commonality extends to other creatures. "Fish, amphibian, and reptile, warm blooded bird and mammals—each of us carries in our veins a salty stream in which the elements sodium, potassium, and calcium are combined in almost the same proportions as sea water," wrote Rachel Carson in *The Sea Around Us.*[31]

Our commonality exists not only in the biological or physical sphere. As I said above, we share culture with at least some other creatures. Other mammals have social patterns and culture—they communicate with one another, enjoy others, care for the youngsters, and have their own educational systems. And we share heart with them. They know what they need for a fulfilling life, and they meet each other at that center of their existence. I have always remembered John Lilly's haunting description of two dolphins that came to the aid of a third, lifting it up to breathe until it could breathe on its own. After describing the process, Lilly commented that if they had been human beings, an observer would have said that spirit was at work, but in dolphins we speak of instinct.[32]

I am less knowledgeable about creatures other than mammals. According to Evelyn Fox Keller, the biologist Barbara McClintock talked and listened to corn. McClintock believed that you must have the patience to "'hear' what the material has to say to you, the openness to 'let it come to you.' Above all, one must have 'a feeling for the organism.'"[33]

And if a part of culture is organizing in order to survive, then corn and other plants may be said to have culture. McClintock concluded: "Organisms have a life and order of their own that scientists can only partially fathom. No models we invent can begin to do full justice to the prodigious capacity of organisms to devise means for guaranteeing their own survival."[34] She found that certain genes move— she named this process "transposition"—in response to stress. And although the significance of this is disputed by some scientists, Keller concluded, "Perhaps the future will show that [the genetic] complexity is such as to enable it not only to program the life cycle of the organism . . . but also to reprogram itself when exposed to sufficient environmental stress—thereby effecting a kind of 'learning' from the organism's experience."[35]

We live in larger wholes, larger patterns. We are dependent on those wholes and are interdependent with the other creatures in them. From the perspective of my commitment to justice and in light of our human capacity to change those wholes, it is imperative to understand ourselves both as being enmeshed in these patterns and as having tremendous responsibility for the changes that our actions produce. We should try neither simply to adjust nor to control. Rather, we have a responsibility both to learn how to live within ecosystems *and* to create change, to help ecosystems evolve toward larger patterns of justice and health for all parts.

We have a responsibility to intervene, but we must do so with all the wisdom we can muster. And wisdom is to be found in a continuing openness to God, to the experiences of those creatures who suffer most from the present patterns, and to our hearts. Taken together, they can tell what is destructive and what is healing. We can also try to learn to speak, heart to heart, with other creatures. And even if we don't all have direct communication with other creatures, we know enough to realize that they need habitat, unpolluted food and water, and freedom and power to live their own lives. And we know that the population of human beings, like that of coyotes or any other creatures, must be limited enough so that others can also survive and indeed so that no species eventually destroys itself because it no longer has food, air, and water for its own survival.

Our ecosystems are givens, that is, we cannot be without them. They are also constructions. They attempt to make sense of some of the world in which we live. As constructions, they are partial, limited, biased. Nevertheless, I believe they are also genuine and valid *responses* to the world in which we live. For me, at least, our ecosystems offer a framework that enables me to hold together and honor the many dimensions of life that are surely being destroyed by the social systems and beliefs that have been erected in the West. They enable me to make sense of what is happening and find direction for alternative social patterns. They enable me to be faithful to the God I love, who is made known to me in Jesus and in the lives of those committed to a more just and whole life for all.

The preceding discussions of social constructions and of species difference and commonality leads me to the awareness of the need for new images for humanity and the natural world in relation to each other. The two major paradigmatic images of nature in the dominant Western culture are both disastrous in that they are both dualistic: they reflect a human–natural world dualism of an ethical—good/bad—dualism. Their elaboration in the nineteenth century, our immediate legacy, also reflects a Victorian hierarchical social construction. The two images are Darwin's, at least as popularized, "nature red in tooth and claw," and Thoreau's more feminine images, with also a "nature as good, culture as bad" dualism.

Historian Donald Worster wrote of Darwin: "Near the end of his life, he was strongly impressed as ever with the universality of violence in man and nature. Noting that 'the Caucasian races have beaten the Turkish hollow in the struggle for existence,' he added that it seemed to be a law of history and progress that an 'endless number of lower races' had to be wiped out by 'the higher civilized races.'"[36] The more romantic imaging of nature, as expressed by Thoreau, for instance, is equally problematic. Thoreau saw nature as mother, nurse, teacher, and lover. "Too early he complained were we 'weaned from her breast to society.'"[37] This feminine imagery was contrasted with the brutality and materialism of civilization. Although Thoreau had a more "positive"—at least, nicer—view of the natural world, he built that view from stereotypical notions of white middle-class women of the nineteenth century and helped to perpetuate the culture-nature dualism that I find lingering today in some ecofeminist theory.

As I think of images that are more appropriate to my construction of creation, I recognize their relativity and hope that they do not inadvertently perpetuate oppressive conditions for others but rather illumine dimensions of creation that can be honored by others. At the same time, it is important to recognize that these images emerge from the experiences of different groups and are not and need not be shared equally by all. Creation is like a prism; images can be facets that can enrich our understanding even as they reflect diverse locations and histories.

I offer six different kinds of images that help me to understand what creation might mean: images of kinship and household; images of oppression, liberation, and birthing; images of alliance or covenant; images of artistry; images of fecundity and plenty; and images of freedom, wildness, strangeness, and mystery. Creatures are the household of God and one another. We are kin of one another and of all that is; we are kin of God. We are part of a large extended family, not a nuclear family and not just a human family! It is, however, a family with no prescribed roles and no hierarchical structure. It is a family in which members quarrel with as well as care for one another.

I prefer "kinship of God" or "household of God" to "city of God" or "kingdom of God." The latter are too exclusively human-focused, and "kingdom" is much too hierarchical. "Kinship" or "household" need not communicate either of these. An extended family can be an ecological unit as well as a human one. And what is powerful about family is that it points to the giveness of our relationships. If we are kin of one another, we have privileges and responsibilities inherent in and as defined by that household. We are sisters and brothers not simply by choice, as we choose friends.

Further, although the image of household does not specify any particular economic arrangement, it is suggestive. Setting an economic discussion in the context of household is quite different from setting it in the current pattern of nation-states and transnational corporations. Creation as household suggests a global economy but one designed to meet the needs of the entire household, not to increase the profits of a few human beings.

Another image that I find increasingly compelling is the biblical one of the whole creation groaning for liberation. In his letter to the Romans, for instance, Paul wrote, "The creation itself will be set free from its bondage . . . and . . . the whole creation has been groaning in labor pains until now" (8:21, 22). The earth, air, water, plants, and other animals and our relationship with them are all caught up in structures of oppression. All should be set free, renewed.

We are kin, but we don't act like kin. We are in bondage, yearning to be free. We are giving birth to ourselves and to one another. Essential to that ongoing transformation is the forming of alliances, for different reasons for people in different social locations. So I find alliance a new and helpful theological image. The more traditional image is covenant. We commit ourselves to one another—to learn, to listen, to share our stories, to work together.

For the immediate future, I prefer alliance to covenant. Covenant assumes an equality and does not necessarily suggest the need for ongoing change and transformation in any or all of the covenanting partners. But as white feminists, we can and should be in a holy alliance with one another for our own salvation as well as for our collective struggle for justice, well-being, and sustainability. We are in an ecological alliance of God. Likewise, God is part of an ecological alliance. God is committed to us and to the rest of creation. The powers of the universe have been pledged to us.

I also find aesthetic images of creation helpful and important. God is an artist, a creator; we are cocreators. We are all involved in an ongoing process of making things out of our yearnings, insights, passions, and skills. Put another way, creation is an ongoing creativity.

Among humankind, aesthetic images include a wide range of activities—gardening, writing, quilting, sculpting, designing a house and building it, opening new horizons in a student's mind and heart. I expect that we are not the only cocreators; I don't think it is stretching the idea too far to say that beavers, for instance, are also cocreators. I anticipate that as we lower the barriers and dualisms between humans and other beings, we will find that at least some of the latter also make things out of a combination of their own forms of intelligence, heart, and skills.

A fifth cluster of images suggests fecundity, plenty. We are resources for one another, and there must be sufficient resources for all. Images of fertility—sexual, agricultural, and oceanic—are age-old evocations and honorings of the richness of creation. Images of lovers delighting in one another—human lovers and hills clapping their hands for joy—evoke and honor the richness of creation.

All of the above clusters of images suggest an intimacy between humanity and the rest of creation. It is vitally important also to maintain a respectful distance from ourselves and the natural world. This is important for at least two reasons: to be aware of and alert to the power of God as mystery in the depths of all creaturely being and to remind us that creation is not ours to control, specifically to remind us that other human and nonhuman beings are not the resources for a few. Images that evoke wildness, freedom, mystery, and even violence illumine this dimension of our lives together. Images of storms, raging surf, volcanoes, and atomic energy evoke untamed nature, strength, and even violence, all of which rightly relativize human endeavors to bring order and security into existence. Similarly, images of bears hibernating and of people learning to build houses away from floodplains evoke a respect for that wildness—living with it, fitting into ecosystems, recognizing the depths of existence that can simultaneously destroy and inspire us.

In light of this relational construction that recognizes difference, commonality, and interdependence, there is no such being as "woman"—in the West, at least. It is an abstraction loaded with political significance for everyone. Nor is there an essential female, some universal quality of womanness, unique to females. Even anatomical, hormonal, and muscular characteristics exist on a continuum with males and are developed or inhibited in light of cultural values and social roles and responsibilities.

We would do well to speak as specifically as we know how when we speak of women, for example, to speak, as I have been trying to do, of white middle-class women or young black lesbian women or whomever we are actually speaking about.

If we have no essence, at least none that we can know at this time in history, we are profoundly free to shape ourselves and to join in mutual shaping according to our visions and values. If we have differences and commonalities, we are free to participate within our social groups and across them in the ongoing creation of human life on earth. We can decide within our own heritages and experiences, within our dreams—but always with an awareness of how our yearnings are related to the yearnings of others—what it means to be this woman or this man.

This is likewise true with nature or the natural world. There are trees and bugs and earth and whales, but we do not have to call them "the environment." Indeed, we should not continue to use the word "environment" or other terms that deny our intrinsic connection with the earth. Nor should we romanticize nature as purer than human existence. Instead, we must learn to live together.

CREATEDNESS MEANS VALUE

To say that we are created is to say that we are valued and valuable. Explicit in any Christian understanding of the world, including a feminist one, is the affirmation that the world is created in love, by love, and for love. Human beings are loved; the natural world is loved. Human beings are valued; the natural world is valued. Human beings are created to love and enjoy one another, all of creation, and God. God as mystery is the source of that love and is, as the various images above suggest, mother, sister, father, brother, friend, womb, sea.

Further, we are valuable. We are not valuable simply because we are created, although that is part of the reason. The first sweater I tried to knit was terrible, but it had a certain value to me as the result of something I had learned to do and had struggled with through to the end. But I think a feminist Christian understanding of creation goes further than that kind of value. To say that we are creatures, created, is to say that we have value, that the sweater is worth wearing. It is warm, has an appealing (some would say outrageous) pattern, and fits. It is a good sweater.

All human beings are valuable—men as well as women, our enemies as well as our friends. All human beings, thus, are to be respected. They are not objects, things, one-dimensional stereotypes. All should be able to express power, be part of loving communities, share in the resources of society, and have opportunities to grow toward maturity and wholeness. They have experiences and visions that can enrich the future. Old women and men are complex human beings, subjects of their own existence, not objects to be manipulated, stereotyped, or cast aside. The same is true of all other groups and individuals.

We may be in opposition to some; we may even be in mortal combat. But our enemies are still human beings, created in love, for love. Our conflict must be set in this larger context.

What is true of humanity is also true of nonhuman beings. They too are valued members of their own communities and the larger ecological communities we share with them. As far as I know, this is as true of mosquitoes and other species we call "pests" as it is of whales and dolphins. They should have what they need to survive and live well.

I recognize, of course, that the wolf does not (yet) lie down with the lamb or with people. But the affirmation of wolves, mosquitoes, and poison ivy as created means that I do not have the right to try to exterminate them simply because they are a nuisance and/or threat to some of my interests or even occasionally to my existence. I have a responsibility not only to find ways to protect myself but also to ask to what extent I am intruding into their lives: do they also have space within this ecosystem to exist and to thrive? If not, what must I do about my own pattern of living to make theirs possible? And I must ask about population, theirs and mine: to what extent do either or both need to be limited?

The affirmation that all creation is valuable is the theological basis for challenging the construction of nature as resource. Nature does not exist to be a resource for human beings, actually for very few human beings. It exists for itself and for the love and enjoyment of one another. It does not belong to us. Indeed, we are part of a larger whole and must learn how to live with that awareness.

As I write this, I realize how nearly impossible it is for so many Americans to grasp this affirmation, although it is easy enough to say. For many, nature as a resource exists as a dream, out of their reach. For others, it exists daily as fact. Our houses, lawns, cars, food, and clothes, our supermarkets, malls, outlets, and specialty stores, our television commercials and programs and home shopping channels all flow together into a mighty river of goods and services. Although this flood is touted as making life better and easier and more efficient, it really ensures that the economy will continue, regardless of its impact on people's lives or on the earth. The effect has been to enable certain groups to live comfortably and creatively (with the institutions of art, music, poetry, and literature), at a distance from nature, and to turn the natural world into consumable goods.

This inundation of propaganda and things obscures the reality that there is an appropriate way for us to understand humanity and the earth as resources for one another. For we are. We are resources for one another. Many birds eat mosquitoes; we can use deer hides; I trust that poison ivy has some usefulness. Any creature that lives uses aspects of the rest of creation. We have to learn that we can and should be resources for others. Our bodies after death should be able to nurture the earth. Our minds and creative spirits can be resources that facilitate the well-being of others— their preservation and their physical and emotional health.

Finally, to say that we are created is to say that human beings do belong. We are not simply an excrudence, a horrible blight in nature. When some people who are deeply committed to ecological concerns cry out that the natural world doesn't need us and indeed would be better off without us, their anger is understandable but misplaced. Not all human beings despoil nature but are despoiled along with nature, as we know if we understand patterns of racism, classism, patriarchy, and other expressions of social oppression and imperialism. Nor is it part of human nature to despoil the natural world; we have been created to be partners with God and the rest of creation to continue the world's creation and re-creation. The time may come when there will be no human beings, just as now other species have become extinct, but our task at the present is to respond in faithfulness to the clear call to do justice, love mercy, and walk humbly with God—and thus learn how to live with the earth, not against it.

CREATION IS NEW CREATION

Learning to live with the earth is participating in the advent of new creation. New creation—the transforming of relationships into healthy, just patterns—continues to be a possibility in and emerges out of present patterns. Creation continues; it can be *new,* that is foreshadowing and witnessing to patterns that Jesus, and many other biblical and nonbiblical women and men, envisioned, lived, and died for.

New creation is now; the kinship, the alliance of God, is now; redemption is now. If creation is ongoing, if it is characterized by change, conflict, and new insights and experiences as ecosocial locations shift, the promised new time of the Bible and the present creation are to some extent synonymous. At least, they occur simultaneously. What emerges can, of course, be as marred as what exists, *but* there is always the possibility that the genesis of different patterns, of different ways of responding, will also emerge. A more just, more healing, more healthy, more liberating, and more strongly surviving touch, gesture, action, or policy—a miracle—may break through and begin to forgive, set us free from, an unjust, unhealthy past.

At the same time, of course, we continue to look to the future, to the promise of a fuller life than what any of us are likely to be experiencing now, trapped as we are in different ways, in the patterns that currently exist. But once again, the future comes from the present, a present imbued with existing patterns in relation to God and thus always open to mystery—and to radical newness as well as the more incremental survivals and changes of daily life.

For Christians, Jesus has been a central figure in and source of the possibility of the movement toward fullness of life, new creation. Specifically, for many, the end of Jesus' life—his death—has been the critical event for making new creation possible. New creation has meant salvation, and the church has claimed that it was God, not just the man Jesus, who died "for us."

This affirmation has been the cornerstone of the church's theology. It has been preserved in countless creeds and confessions. It has been argued over and fought over. Its implications have been addressed and elaborated ad infinitum. It has served many social and political purposes, some justice-making, others justice-denying, at least from my perspective today. Many womanists and feminists have criticized dimensions of it because it has helped to justify war and violence, to promote a tyrannical understanding of power, to deny our human embodied existence, to justify religious, economic, and political imperialism, to perpetuate black women's surrogacy, and in general to support the social powerlessness of most people. I accept and agree with those charges. I explored some of them in previous chapters. In sum, I find this theological cornerstone morally disastrous.

In a critical passage in *Sisters in the Wilderness,* Delores Williams wrote:

> Jesus showed humankind a vision of righting relations between body, mind and spirit *through an ethical ministry of word* (such as the beatitudes, the parables, the moral directions and reprimands); *through a healing ministry of touch and being touched* (for example, healing the leper through touch; being touched by the woman with and issue of blood); *through a militant ministry of expelling evil forces* (such as exorcising the demoniacs, whipping the moneychangers out of the temple); *through a ministry grounded in the power of faith* (in the work of healing); *through a ministry of prayer* (he often withdrew from the crowd to pray); *through a ministry of compassion and love.*
>
> Humankind is, then, redeemed through Jesus' *ministerial* vision of life and not through his death.[38]

As Williams has done, I have shifted the focus of the theological and ethical significance of Jesus to his life and away from his death. The crucifixion is a witness to violence, cruelty, and injustice. It is not a witness to redemption. Again, Williams wrote: "The image of Jesus on the cross is the image of human sin in its most desecrated. . . .The cross thus becomes an image of defilement."[39]

The death of Jesus can have meaning, however. It can be deeply comforting to know that he knows suffering when we suffer, particularly as we are engaged as he was. This in no way justifies the suffering, of course. Suffering is not redemptive. Suffering should be protested, challenged—and overcome.

The death of Jesus can also help illumine evil. People and other beings are killed daily, spiritually and/or physically, through the violence of others and the systems in which we live. Jesus died at the hands of a violent system also. The cross is a reminder of the violence of so much of the world.

And third, insofar as we benefit, at least to some extent, from a society of violence—even as we decry the violence—the cross should call us to conversion. It should call us to live with others toward a future of justice and abundant life for all creation. It should call us to live with others, as those first fruits to which Paul referred.

If Jesus' death is not redemptive, what is the significance of the resurrection? It is important first to distinguish between death as an evil event and death as a natural event. Death is a part of life, and all things being equal, lives follow a process of growth, maturity, and decline to death. Resurrection is not the answer to that process. Resurrection, theologically speaking, is a response—in hope—to death as evil. It is an image of the possibility that new life can come from the old, an old that is structured into oppression and violence.

This is actually affirmed by the biblical record. The resurrection stories are different from the calling forth of Lazarus, who returned to earthly existence. They testify to a new experience of the abiding spirit and power of Jesus, largely in and with the community of those who had been with him during his life.

And the presence of community is critical. I find that the theological significance of resurrection can be seen more clearly if we look at it in relation to Pentecost, if we tie it to the beginnings of the Christian community rather than to Jesus' life. The experience of resurrection was the experience of meeting Jesus spiritually. In these meetings Jesus was known as the Christ, and the Gospel accounts were told and written in light of these meetings. They were Easter, whenever and wherever they took place. Only later did the church think of Easter as a specific time. The resurrection experiences were closely followed by the Pentecost story, the pouring out of the Holy Spirit in the last days, when not only the disciples but also people of culturally diverse backgrounds could understand the church's message about Jesus. It was a period of radicalizing, a time of mystical encounters with God and of tremendous recognition of the holy truth in the life and mission of Jesus as conceptualized in the language and images of the times. Jesus was the Messiah, the Christ. Jesus' life and death ushered in the Messianic period. The story of the church and the story the church has to tell begin with the experiences of God in what we now call resurrection and Pentecost and then move back to Jesus and its own founding.

Those experiences, then, were direct encounters with the spirit of God, with the power of God to give courage, energy, and understanding. They were the beginnings of a series of experiences that continued to nurture and empower the early church. Paul experienced them and became a major leader. Others experienced them particularly in times of crisis and imprisonment. What became Communion, the Lord's Supper, or Mass in later times may have started as not only a remembering but also an experiencing of this spirit we call holy.

The experience of the risen Jesus was so closely tied to life in the church that Paul imaged the church as the body of the Christ. The image is an organic one; the head and the rest of the body cannot be separated without death to both. It is interesting that the story of Paul's conversion, as told in Acts, has Jesus asking him why he was persecuting Jesus, not why he was persecuting the church. The risen Christ and the church are intrinsically joined.

Feminist theologians have generally affirmed this connection, although they redefine "church." Separating the historical person Jesus from the Christ, they write that Christ, the redemptive presence of God, is present in many people and even events, including those outside the institution. Kelly Brown Douglas understands the Christ as one who challenges the "Black community to rid itself of anything that divides it against itself and to renounce any way in which it oppresses others." Christ can thus be seen in women and men who have so expressed God's will.[40] Jacquelyn Grant wrote: "God becomes concrete not only in the man Jesus, for he was crucified, but in the lives of those who will accept the challenges of the risen Saviour the Christ. For Lee, this meant that women could preach; for Sojourner, it meant that women could possibly save the world; for me, it means today, this Christ, found in the experiences of Black women, is a Black woman."[41]

Some emphasize Christ as a social reality. Rosemary Ruether has written that Christ must not be "encapsulated" in the historical Jesus. Rather, Christ, "as redemptive person and Word of God," is continued in the Christian community. "As vine and branches Christic personhood continues in our sisters and brothers."[42] Rita Nakashima Brock also understands Christ in social terms but much more fully than Ruether. Even in Jesus' lifetime, what is redemptive about him is the community of which he was a part, the relationships of what she names "erotic power." "The Christa/Community of erotic power is the connectedness among the members of the community who live with heart."[43]

Elizabeth Johnson summarized much of this effort: "Jesus has truly died. . . . His life is now hidden in the glory of God, while his presence is known only through the Spirit where two or three gather, bread is broken, the hungry fed."[44] In Johnson's words, "Christ is a pneumatological reality, a creation of the Spirit who is not limited by whether one is Jew or Greek, slave or free, male or female."[45]

These constructions do not draw on apocalyptic images of Christ and the coming of God's realm in any significant way. Townes, however, does return to them "to offer an alternative picture of reality and point the community in that direction."[46] As in the early church, so today for African Americans, an apocalyptic vision arises from persecution, from suffering and martyrdom. It is a vision that rejects utterly this present condition; it is a vision of God's "no" to injustice and a hope of a new heaven and earth.

Apocalyptic imagery lifts up the church as over-against culture, both the white dominant culture and the infiltration of that culture into the black community. It enables the church to understand that every dimension of life must be questioned. Townes wrote:

> The nature of the apocalypse leaves no part of our lives unscathed. From the reality of lynching—be it by rope, by environment, or by political ideology—to our images of gender and sexuality, to our search for identity and the ongoing negative impact of colorism, to the African American class structure and our struggles with poverty and the underclass, we are community that is under siege from forces outside us and forces within. The Black Church must reclaim and live out a spirituality that is its social witness.[47]

Townes contrasts and holds in tension a prophetic and apocalyptic eschatology. In the former she sees God acting through human beings and events; in the latter, God as Christ is in some sense still to come—"in a blaze of glory," as the title of her book testifies. This means that there is a strong emphasis on the work that the church, specifically the black church, must do to be the church, to name clearly and honestly the forces that besiege it from without but also from within. And she takes another daring step. She reminds her readers that the cross comes before resurrection and thus that African Americans are called to a witness that may mean their lives, a witness that she recognizes is risky as well as difficult when they are already cast into the role of victims in this country. Nevertheless, the church must address the issues that tear black people apart as well as those that assault them from the dominant structure. As black people seek to live into their witness, they will "find God waiting for us and also prodding us into wholeness as individuals, as a people, as a church. It is in this glory that womanist spirituality finds its witness."[48]

I find connecting resurrection and Pentecost to be an extremely insightful theological approach. This connection sets resurrection free from its tie to a specific event in the past, to the empty tomb and to the contradictory and problematic accounts in the Gospels of how embodied the risen Jesus was. More important, it helps to reconfigure the center: God is present today as God was present centuries ago. We are not only the inheritors of traditions; we are also contemporaries of Mary Magdalene, Joanna, Paul, and the disciples on the Emmaus road. We too can experience the spirit of God ablaze in Jesus, inspiring and empowering us to begin new traditions. We too can experience of the energy of God, swirling around the foundations of our lives, creating new patterns for our lives together.

Salvation, thus, is an ongoing, multifaceted, interrelated activity. It includes movements of survival and protest; of liberation from patterns of oppression and power; of transformation toward well-being, sustainability, and justice. Salvation neither began with Jesus nor ended with him. He was certainly a participant in it, and he remains a symbol to Christians of what is saving or redemptive. And he affirms that God remains with us in our struggle toward new creation.

Further, this approach emphasizes resurrection as a political reality and thus complements the seasonal images and celebrations of solstice and equinox, planting and harvesting. The disciples fled when Jesus was killed and came back together when they met his spirit; so too we become demoralized, overwhelmed, and tired, but then something happens and we are renewed and we continue the struggle. Just as the early church attempted to structure itself in fidelity to Jesus' vision and life, so new communities can rise on the edges of the old. The early church shared bread and wine, the staples of peasant life; the people shared their resources and lived in the presence of the spirit that they named Jesus the Christ. So too we can come together from the brokenness of our lives and the forces that separate us and that make us enemies. The dividing walls of hostility can be shattered, making one new community in which we learn what it means to become friends. That is truly resurrection.

Finally, connecting resurrection and Pentecost reaffirms resurrection as a powerful image of hope: love and justice are stronger than their denial in all areas of life—personal, interpersonal, political, and spiritual-bodily. Love and justice may not be as inevitable as the profusion of zucchini that follows the planting of seeds, but they are possible, available. And we can put ourselves in a position to participate in our own and others' resurrection. We can be generous. We can learn to forgive, that is, not simply to respond in kind but to introduce a new, creative response that moves us beyond where we are and opens up new ways of relating and of addressing conflicts.[49] We can put ourselves in a position to respond to generosity and creativity. If we are open to the powers of the universe—to God and to one another and to the earth—we will be resurrected, and we will participate in the resurrecting of others.

As I reflect on resurrection, I also find myself agreeing with what Townes wrote about the importance of apocalyptic eschatology, although for quite different reasons. I am extremely cautious about locating Christ within the church. I see so much about the white church that is a travesty and trivialization of Jesus' life and ministry. I sometimes have an image of Jesus returning as a twentieth-century American who walks into a white church on a Sunday morning and flees in horror.

The same caution holds when I think of church as a community of those largely white people who covenant to be faithful to a God calling us to witness to new creation. Our history is one of continuing temptation to arrogance, to a belief that we know what is right and true for the world. The only places in which I can identify the healing, redemptive power of God—symbolized in the title of Christ—is in movements toward relationships of honesty, respect, alliance, and listening and, within those movements, in commitments to justice. The formerly mainline institutional church can be a context within which such relationships can be experienced.

But this church is also far from embodying them. It is far from being the body of Christ. Like the world, this church needs ongoing conversion before such relationships become part of the fabric of our lives.

CREATION AND SIN

The traditional way to talk about sin is to locate it between creation and redemption or new creation. I have changed the order to stress the connection between creation and new creation and to throw into relief how we might understand sin and evil.

Sin and evil were very real in my Presbyterian heritage. They were not presented to me as something I had to be vigilant about every day, or at least I did not hear that message if it was given. But neither were they simply a backdrop to Christ's victory on the cross. The cross, resurrection, and sin and evil were all like solid, functional pieces of furniture in the living room of God's house (i.e., world). They existed, and we were to take due notice of them as we negotiated our paths among them.

Sin and evil remain very real. Most of this book speaks about them and our response to them. They name the reality we live in. Oppression and violence are basic to any feminist or womanist understanding of theology. Williams, for instance, defines sin in terms of the devaluation of African American women's humanity and the defilement of their bodies by a racist, patriarchal system.[50]

Evil and sin name both historical patterns of domination, oppression, and violence *and* personal attitudes, beliefs, and actions. Sin is, therefore, social and systemic. It is not ontological, some inherited fault that each of us is born with. At the same time, sin precedes us; in a historical sense, it is original, since we are born into patterns that violate and destroy the earth and its inhabitants. So racism is sin. Some have named it this country's original sin. Patriarchy is sin. Classism is sin. Heterosexism is sin. Ageism is sin. Ableism is sin. The exploitation and destruction of the earth is sin. They are not the only patterns we are born into. As I have just written, we also experience love, forgiveness, respect, community—patterns of relationships that nurture and cherish and build us up. But we are born also into patterns that violate and destroy us.

To name sin in this way is to recognize that it is not experienced in the same way by all people. The sin I am addressing is very much an expression of a white, Western dominant social pattern—supported and reinforced by military might. It names very specific patterns of domination and violence and the different ways those patterns are experienced by people and the earth in different ecosocial locations. It names specific patterns and the extent to which individuals and different groups support those patterns. Sin is not generically pride or alienation or any other one way of being in the world.

Many of the structures of sin come together in very concrete data. Of the world's population, 20 percent control 83 percent of the world's wealth, whereas the 20 percent of the world's poorest population, mostly people of color, control less than 1.5 percent. And 18 percent of all full-time jobs in the United States do not pay enough to raise families above poverty. And 5 to 8 percent of the U.S. population are *never* able to find jobs because of the way the economy is structured. And . . . and . . . and . . .[51] This is sinful. This is evil. This pattern causes extreme suffering and violence to people who have no real say in the decisions that lead to these consequences.

Further, such a pattern both reflects and perpetuates the belief that some people are superior to others and to the natural world—superior in value and being. For instance, dominants, those who are in charge or aspire to be in charge, have a good work ethic, are more productive, make something of their lives, are the good citizens of a community, and implicitly or explicitly, are more intelligent than the others. In short, for those of us so privileged, sin is what is normal. In extreme cases, sin has become so deeply entrenched in one that it has led to the death of one's heart.

Sin may be knowledgeable and malicious. Actions, policies, and patterns may be created and perpetuated deliberately to discriminate against, make marginal, and destroy the lives and/or spirits of others. But sin may be much more unconscious or indifferent. As Hannah Arendt identified in her classic analysis of the Eichmann trial, evil can be banal.[52] It is expressed in conducting "business as usual," in "doing our duty." It is expressed in indifference and callousness toward others when we are in positions of power and authority. It is expressed in policies and laws that reflect this indifference and callousness. A recent study in Maine showed that the median income for *all* women was a little over $7 an hour and that the cost for a family of three (one parent and two children) to live was over $11 an hour.[53] The median income for men is something over $12 an hour. Since most single parents are women, it is not surprising that many are on welfare. That pattern is evil, and what makes it even worse is that one state legislator seriously proposed that after a woman had been on welfare for three years, she not only had to get off but could *never be on again.* The legislator has the same figures that I do; the figures have been widely publicized, and legislators have been repeatedly lobbied with such information. The legislator's indifference is simply the sin of callousness.

Williams named sin for African American women as what they experience at the hands of the dominant culture. It is not something they are guilty of. For her, black women become guilty if or when they accept the stereotypical images of black womanhood or do not challenge patterns and policies that defile black women's bodies "through physical violence, sexual abuse and exploited labor."[54]

How should we, as white women, name sin, its effects on us, and our participation in it? Naming sin as systemic oppression, unearned advantage, and social power over others on the one hand theologically frees us from the inheritance that we are somehow sinful because we are female or if we dare to claim that we should care for ourselves as well as others. It frees us from the burden of servanthood and sacrifice, from low self-esteem and feelings of unworthiness. At the same time, naming sin in this way holds us accountable to address the ways in which we as white women are complicit in maintaining destructive patterns. It recognizes that we live in the midst of complex and contradictory structures and that we have a responsibility to address the ways in which they all shape our lives and our relationships with the earth and its inhabitants.

For us, therefore, sin is experienced in many specific ways. It is experienced in violence directed at us. Rape, incest, harassment, and demeaning and contemptuous images threaten, violate, or destroy us. Sin is experienced in my own pain and need, which twists and undercuts my love and enjoyment of myself and others. It is experienced in my silence and misdirected anger—too often turned inward.

Sin is experienced in the way it subverts the possibility of mutuality with anyone—men of my own race and class, women of any race and class. I may live literally in a no-man's-land, among other women and with children. But taught that my interests lie with men, I find it difficult to relate as equals, in mutual respect and care, to other women and certainly to the women who work in "man's land" or who work for me and for others like me, primarily in dependent positions and for barely surviving or nonsurvival pay.

Similarly, if I work outside the home, I and others bring these internalized attitudes with me. In addition, the dominant culture's sexualization of women's being, along with fears about sexuality, dramatically inhibit the possibilities of moving toward friendships with either women or men.

But sin for us is also expressed in other ways. It is experienced in holding onto the financial security that the status quo offers, in seeking advancement within the status quo as if we have totally "earned" it, in believing that our interests are recognized and upheld by white middle-class men, in believing that what we have and who we are represent the norm, and in refusing to use the power given us by our race and class membership for change.

And it is experienced in ignoring the pain, need, and promise of other beings as well as in being cruel to them. Insofar as we have internalized the stereotypes and mythologies of the dominant culture and our connection with white men, we not only remain separated and alienated from others who are oppressed; we also don't care about them or even actively do violence to them. Our socialization to be nurturers comes with significant boundaries. What is so often missing is the courage to name our location and to use and to risk what we have for justice and the welfare of all, including ourselves.

We—white, middle-class feminists—are in an interesting, ambiguous, and challenging place. We must continue to learn the landscape in its uniqueness as well as in its similarities to where others live. If we are to be "saved," we must open ourselves to the God of challenge and resistance to our privilege as well as to our oppression.

STRUGGLE AND TRANSFORMATION

Above, I wrote that Jesus saves us by sharing his vision of what he called "the kingdom" and what I call "new creation." He sets us free to develop it, adapt it, change it, and bring it closer to fruition. It is as if he says to us: "This is what I envision, given where I stood. Now it's your turn."

Those of us who have pledged fidelity to that early vision and to the God who inspired it must find ways to share our own particular visions and to find and develop common visions even as we maintain the richness and challenge of diverse ones. None of us can know what new creation might look like generations from now except at the level of principle—that is, it will be a more just society, one that is more sustainable, one in which all live well, one shaped by mutuality and respect. But we can envision approximations, given our best wisdom and diverse experience within the options that we can even imagine today. In that spirit, I now turn to a consideration of the Christian life that seeks to bear witness to transformation.

"You shall love the Sovereign your God with all your heart, and with all your soul, and with all your strength, and with all your mind; and your neighbor as yourself. You shall love the Sovereign your God with all your heart, and with all your soul, and with all your strength, and with all your mind; and your neighbor as yourself."

5

TRANSFORMING LIFE IN THE WORLD

Enabling people to . . . recover a capacity to long for
economic justice as deeply as we desire political justice is
the task of religious ethics today.
                    —*Beverly Harrison, in* Making the Connections

As Christians, we live in faithfulness to God and her presence in the world. We live not simply "between the times," but in witness to new creation and in struggle to anticipate it. We live in tension, pain, and joy amid Jesus' vision and life, our visions and our responsibilities and possibilities.

In this chapter, I will explore in more detail our lives as Christians. First, I will theoretically examine patterns of decision-making, what is often thought of under the rubric "Christian ethics." Then I will turn to a discussion of personal, interpersonal, and social transformation—our bearing, or presence in the world. This dimension of the Christian life has traditionally been called "virtue" or "character." Following those two, I will turn to explorations of economic life: our relationships with other creatures and our relationships to ourselves. How might we shape this area of institutions so that it is more open to the transformative power of God, to new creation?

DECISION-MAKING

Much of traditional philosophical and theological ethics has focused on making decisions—determining the right action to take or the action to achieve some good. A post-Christendom feminist ethic agrees with much other feminist-womanist reflection that we come to questions about decisions embedded in relationships. We are already in relations in which we made specific commitments and pledged loyalties, as well as in the broader relations of oppression, privilege, power, and conflict. Further, as Christians, we are in relationships of struggle and conflict toward change and even transformation.

When this relational and changing pattern is understood as the context and condition of Christian ethics, then ethics itself changes. To a lesser or greater extent, we create new moralities. This kind of change has, of course, happened many times, although it has not always been acknowledged. The church has created a number of new moralities of sexuality, for instance. Apparently, gay and lesbian people were accepted as Christian and held church offices for several centuries. Graves in which same-sex couples have been buried are numerous, and ceremonies uniting same-sex couples date up to the tenth or eleventh century. Economic ethics, ethics of war, political ethics, and ethics of the family have all changed throughout the many years of Christian history. These changes are connected with different ecosocial locations, different insights into the Bible, different relationships with and understandings of Jesus, and different patterns of reflection on Christian life in the world. There is no reason to assume that those changes will or should cease now. Indeed, we drastically need some new ethics!

A relational approach to Christian ethics is significantly different from much of traditional ethics. It questions much of what has been considered absolute in ethics. It does not begin with an unchanging natural law or assume some moral absolutes. It challenges the image of the moral agent as standing in isolation at some moral crossroads. It challenges the pattern in which elites within the church, whether Catholic or Protestant, determine what is right or good for the rest of us. And it also challenges some dimensions of ethics based on a more contemporary model of relationality.

In the past, Christians have often regarded the Bible as an absolute or as the interpreter of God's absolute will. The model I propose takes biblical material seriously but severely relativizes its authoritative role. As I wrote earlier, the Bible contributes to our decision-making. For me, Jesus is a touchstone, as is Scripture in general. The images and stories of the Bible offer a wealth of insights, discoveries, and challenges when I open my heart and mind to them, but I do not proof-text, and I am very much aware that there is much in Scripture that has been used to oppress groups of people and the earth. Nor do I lift up a sense of the general tenor of Jesus' vision and ministry or the whole life of Jesus as *the* authority of ethics. Jesus is a compelling and inspiring figure, but I consider it idolatry to attribute to him a prescience that denies his humanity. Jesus is a holy person; he is not an ahistorical being.

A relational approach to ethics recognizes that personal decisions are intrinsically related to political ones. Our relationships are embedded in institutional and cultural patterns of power, privilege, and violence. So what may seem like personal decisions are related to the struggle for justice, well-being, and sustainability. How I live my life is not only a personal matter, unrelated to and in isolation from either ecosocial location or new creation. How I understand myself as a sexual being, what I do with my money or lack of it, what I do with "spare time" (would that I had some!), how I relate to others—all of these and more are set within both ecological, historical-social contexts and ecological, historical-social contexts that are coming into being.

The understanding of Christian ethics I am proposing is dynamic, pluralistic, and communal. The "right thing to do" *emerges* out of a process that may be intentional or more intuitive. We look to Jesus and the rest of Scripture; we look to one another, to our ecosocial locations, commitments, alliances, and experiences; we reach out to others' experiences, insights, and commitments and to people who live out of different ecosocial locations; we look to relevant and appropriate reflection of the church; we look to stories and empirical data; we look to reasoned analysis and reflection; we look to the principles of justice, sustainability, and well-being. And we often struggle to decide on a particular course of action or a whole series of actions. The decision emerges out of that process. If we are faithful to the process, the decision will be as "right" as it can be.

On some occasions, we will go through each part of the process consciously and carefully. On other occasions, the process will be much more intuitive or internal to the individual. As members of the Bath UCC church struggle toward becoming an "open and affirming" church, that is, one publicly welcoming gay, lesbian, and bisexual people, we are in effect following that process.

Often the relational context and condition of our decision-making will be conflict-filled, with competing claims on us. Often the nature of the conflicts is such that very possibly the "right thing to do" will cost us, particularly cost dimensions of advantage and power. Ensuring that the relationality within our decision-making framework includes alliances with people in quite different ecosocial locations enables us to recognize and even embrace the conflicts and challenges and holds us accountable as we wrestle with making appropriate decisions.

In any given situation, therefore, a decision is not a reflection or approximation of an ideal good, rightness, or justice. Rather, it is a response of survival, a piecemeal correction to massive injustice and/or at best a tiny step in transformation toward justice. And each response, correction, or step is itself subject to distortion, bias, and further tragedy and evil.

Decision-making, in other words, seems to me to be thoroughly ambiguous. So much so that I wonder to what extent it even makes sense to speak of "doing the right or good action." And yet the imperative to "love mercy, do justice and walk humbly with God" must be central to us. If we are to be responsible in the decisions we make, we are driven to ever-deeper relationships with God and with one another across boundaries of difference.

CHRISTIAN PRESENCE

The more I think about and try to live a Christian life, the more aware I become of the need for what has been called "Christian nurture," or an ethic of virtue. The more the values, awarenesses, and understandings, as well as the loyalties and spiritual depths explored in this book, become part of people's identity, the better prepared they/we are for the witness and work of a post-Christendom church.

As I think about an ethic of virtue, however, I am aware that traditionally it has assumed a linear model of development. Virtues are described, particularly those called "cardinal," and people are urged to achieve them or reach them in some way, including through grace. In this model, inevitably, some people are more virtuous than others.

This model also has assumed a construction of human nature that I called into question in a previous chapter. We are not like acorns that will become oak trees if nurtured appropriately. We do not have an abstract, timeless human essence that ultimately denies the ethical significance of our historical and social differences.

Further, theologians appropriated Greek and Latin excellences of the male citizen and added to them or transformed them with valued Christian traits of character. Justice, wisdom, temperance, and courage were identified by Plato as necessary for the ideal *polis;* Augustine made them into theological virtues.

Nor are we corrupted, willful beings who need restoration to our "true" nature and simultaneously to God, often through some kind of discipline or control. Theologians in Christendom might assume (and did) that everyone should know God and be obedient to "Him" by nature and that the virtuous Christian lived a life of obedience, one in which the self obeyed God and the emotions obeyed reason and/or the body obeyed the spirit (and, in general, inferiors obeyed superiors). In such an understanding of the Christian life, the traditional virtues became gifts. Love, for instance, became *caritas* or *agape,* not our earthly *eros* directed to God and the neighbor.

If we don't have a *nature,* an *essence,* and if a feminist construction of the universe is nonhierarchical, how might we think of virtue and of nurturing the development of a certain kind of self? I suggest we begin with where we are and what we need. Our "virtues," our excellences, will vary somewhat, depending on ecosocial location and its intersection with the call to be faithful.

African American womanists have identified character traits important to their struggle for survival, resistance, and justice. M. Shawn Copeland speaks of "sass," along with courage and mother wit, which enabled slaves to resist.[1] Similarly, in her study of Ida Wells-Barnett, Emilie Townes wrote that Wells-Barnett engaged "in outrageous, audacious, courageous or *willful* behavior."[2] That kind of behavior was in part a prophetic response to the injustices she fought, but it also grew out of a disposition, a bearing in the world, that developed over a lifetime of struggle and resistance.

What do we, as middle-class white women, want and need in our struggle? I have chosen to focus on courage and respect in part because they have traditionally been part of the Western male discussion of virtue and in part because I think we need both to appropriate and reconstruct them. Much emphasis has been placed on what (white) women's traditional socialization can contribute to human relationships, on what is valuable in (white) men's socialization that has sometimes been overlooked. Cooperation has been lauded and competition decried, for instance. I generally agree that much of what we have learned is valuable for more peaceful and just human relationships and indeed is necessary for human and the earth's survival. Nevertheless, it is important to integrate and transform those traditional qualities with some others, ones that have been assigned largely to men in this culture. So I will examine courage and respect.

We white middle-class feminist and other women need courage, specifically the courage to express anger, to speak out, and to accept forgiveness. We need to be able to accept and initiate conflict. We have been socialized, at least women of my generation have, to smooth over conflict, to forgive, and to be understanding and pleasant. That kind of presence is certainly important and valuable, but it can severely limit us and serve to help maintain the status quo. If we are to become part of new creation, we must learn ways of challenging old creation, including those patterns in ourselves and others that inhibit the new.

Courage is nurtured by both love and anger. Indeed, these are two sides of the same coin, but since the latter is more problematical for many of us, I will focus this discussion on anger.[3] Speaking out and expressing anger enables us to acknowledge buried dimensions of ourselves. We simply cannot live under the conditions imposed on and expected of us without being wounded and experiencing anger. We cannot read a paper or watch the news without being outraged at the violence and exploitation done to human beings and the natural world. Unless we are dead—that is, our hearts have died—we are angry.

If our anger remains buried, we are cut off from parts of ourselves. We are all familiar with some of the consequences of unacknowledged anger—illness, depression, bitterness, hostility directed toward other women (what psychologists call "horizontal anger"). Buried anger makes it more difficult to be open to healing, to participate in the well-being that is part of new creation. It also cuts us off from the voice of God. We *should* be angry; anger is one of the ways we say that the emperor has no clothes. Anger is absolutely essential if we are to be part of the first fruits of new creation.

There are subtle differences of connotation and, according to Webster, of meaning among such terms as "anger," "hatred," "rage," and "wrath," although I think we often use many of them as synonyms or to distinguish degrees of intensity. I certainly use "rage" as an intense expression of anger. "Wrath" suggests to me an added punitive dimension, which is appropriate at times.

Probably the most troublesome word is "hatred." As Christians we have been taught to love our enemies as well as our neighbors. Where is there room for hating them? I understand hatred both as a very intense and as a more total expression and direction of anger than conveyed by the word "anger" itself. I may be angry at someone, but I don't hate her. If I do come to hate her, I want nothing to do with her at all; I am unwilling to work on those aspects that anger me. Instead, I want distance from her, I want revenge, and/or I want her destroyed.

I think it is absolutely necessary to be able to hate, to feel that intensity of emotion, to grasp that something is so deeply wrong, sinful, or evil. If loving intensely, creating intensely, and playing intensely are good, positive dimensions of living well, so is hating intensely. I think it was Martin Buber who wrote that indifference, not hatred, is the opposite of love. In hating, we care; we care deeply.

It is also necessary to understand why we hate and to learn to respond in diverse ways. As I talk about hatred with other women, I hear that on many occasions, hatred is related to real or perceived powerlessness, often compounded by fear—that is, someone or some system, for example, the welfare system, is imposing unfair and dehumanizing restrictions on me or is abusing or even terrorizing me, and I seem to have no way out. Insofar as is possible, an appropriate response is to organize or to seek support in ways that empower me to get out, to restrain the bondage or terror, and/or to change the system rather than to seek revenge or destruction.

Or the person or system may be judged so evil that it must be destroyed. I think many women and men of my generation thought of Hitler and Nazism that way. A decade later, many came to see communism in that way.

Individuals or groups who have power and privilege can come to hate another person, group, or system because it poses a threat to that power or privilege. I think of the Ku Klux Klan, for instance, or of a business leader who comes to hate groups that have been successful at restricting his or her freedom to continue to pollute the rivers near a factory.

The emotion arises because one sees and feels intense wrong. What one does, how one responds, has to be assessed in light of our commitment to justice and an understanding of how a specific individual or practice is related to a larger whole—a structure. Then I can respond in a twofold way: to the specific incident, if there is one; and to the structural underpinning. The response of the business leader and the response of a woman being abused should be very different. The business leader may need conversion and another way of being powerful. The abused woman may need to find her voice.

But seeking revenge is not necessarily inappropriate either. The longing for justice that lies deep in our hearts has a dimension that yearns for satisfaction as well as transformation. If I have been hurt and hurt and hurt, I appropriately want satisfaction of some kind. It may be public disclosure—both making my story available to others and naming the sources or those perpetrating the injury. It may be financial compensation. Or it may be some kind of legal punishment, short of death.

Thus hatred, as an intense response to wrongs, does and should exist. What we do with it depends on its relation to justice. Hatred clues us to the presence of severe injustice; it serves as a call to resist. How we name the injustice and determine our resistance depends on many factors, not simply the presence of hate.

A correlate of anger is a willingness to put ourselves in a situation where we risk the anger of others toward us. We so often want everyone to be nice. We want to help others (and we want them to appreciate that help). But being nice and helping are not building alliances. Building alliances makes us vulnerable to the suspicion and anger of others. Building alliances confronts us with decisions about moving to the margins of society and/or using what power and privilege we have closer to the centers. It dislocates us. There is such a temptation for white middle-class women to "pick up our toys and go home." The fact that we can do this is a tremendous unearned privilege. If we feel that we are not appropriately appreciated, we can withdraw. We don't (yet) have to stay in the struggle. We can instead sit at our living-room window and write a letter to Congress, or we can collect cast-off furniture for a shelter, without exposing ourselves to misunderstanding, despair, frustration, anger, or even the violence of others. (This is, of course, not at all to say that writing letters to Congress and collecting furniture for shelters are unimportant activities.)

Finally, learning to be courageous does not mean that we should abandon tactfulness, diplomacy, and sensitivity to others. We can speak on our own behalf, speak out against injustice and harm, and speak to hold another accountable and still recognize that we are speaking with people who are also loved by God. But now, as we seek to bring these together, the more traditional qualities are beginning to be grounded not in fear or the need to placate but in the glimpses of a profound and fierce love of God and her creation that so deeply honors the world that we *must* speak, we *must* risk—even our lives.

Courage: can we nurture courage in ourselves and others? How can we do this? Pondering these questions leads me back to the church and to other communities engaged in the struggle for justice, sustainability, and well being. It is difficult to become courageous by oneself. One needs support, encouragement, examples, and people to share uncertainties and fears. The church can nurture courage in its members, specifically its white, middle-class women members.

This is done in many ways. One way is to model courage. There are white middle-class women who are courageous, and they should be acknowledged and celebrated. Opportunities should be given for sharing their stories and struggles, not just putting the women on a pedestal that seems unreachable to others.

Individuals are where they are. One woman may be living with a batterer; another may be concerned about the homeless and may thus be active in Habitat for Humanity; still another may not yet have addressed being molested by her father when she was seven. Or all three of those characteristics may be true for the same woman. A nurturing community can help such a woman begin to name the exploitation or violence, or part of the violence, that is occurring and to do so in a very safe environment. It can also help her name the courage she does have—giving birth to a child, standing up for a friend who was maligned, sending a check to Greenpeace and risking her husband's disapproval, getting out of bed when she would rather lie there with the covers over her head. The community can then stay with that woman as she explores what to do, how to act, and how to continue to explore and act. It can help the woman to make connections between her experiences and the experiences of other groups and also to begin to understand the structural connections.

Clearly, people will respond in different ways and around different issues. One may handcuff herself to government gates, as some of our foremothers have done. But another may decide to leave her husband; for her, that may be a tremendous act of courage. Another, after addressing her anger and guilt, may say to an aging parent, "I can't take care of you at home any longer." Still another will read Delores Williams's *Sisters in the Wilderness* and create a discussion group that leads to an ongoing anti-racism working group in the church.

This kind of nurture can and should begin in childhood. Courage can be celebrated and encouraged in children as well as in adults (and in men as well as in women, although the exploration will be somewhat different). Again, much can be done through sharing stories, the children's own and those of others. Again, the point is not to impose a model on children—not everyone need be Joan of Arc—but rather to name and celebrate children's courage, to help them relate their faith and loyalties to ways of being courageous and simply being valued members of a community that takes a stand for what it believes.

A second excellence is respect. This is a very traditional one, but I think white middle-class women both need it and have new dimensions to contribute to it. A feminist appropriation of respect includes both recognizing oneself and others as ends, as creations of God, as beings who have intrinsic value *and* recognizing the consideration, regard, and graciousness that so many of us have grown up with.

A respectful person attends to oneself. Self-respect includes recognizing one's own yearnings and needs, affirming that one is of intrinsic worth, and valuing one's own well-being as equal to the well-being of others. A self-respectful person recognizes her anger and expresses it; she seeks her own good in the context of a common good; she recognizes that pain and even tragedy are a part of our lives together, and although she tries to minimize pain both to others and to herself, avoidance is not the most important consideration in decision-making. Rather, she struggles through pain and tragedy, as necessary, in her commitment to be responsible for and to others, herself, and God.

A respectful person listens to and attends to others. She does not, or tries not to, stereotype others or trivialize who others are and what they say and do. She takes others seriously. A respectful person, precisely because she respects others, also seeks to hold them accountable. She tries to understand why someone acted as she or he did but also recognizes where the other must take responsibility for what was said or done. This requires courage, but it also deepens the regard and graciousness that may come more "naturally." Holding others accountable, challenging them, does not have to take the form of "putting them down" or emotionally trying to destroy them. It can be done by recognizing that the other is acting out of his or her own ecosocial location and experience and is loved and continues to be created by God.

A respectful attitude should and can extend toward the whole of creation, not just toward human beings. This attitude is a deep and attentive regard for plants, animals, and the earth, a recognition that they too are ends in themselves, beings with intrinsic value.

So many traditional "housewifely" values are included in respect toward the whole of creation. I think of the thriftiness, for instance, of my grandmother, who saved string, used and reused containers, shopped for goods that would last, and handed down clothes from one member of the family to another. She may have done so for economic reasons (or not), but her actions are an expression of respecting the earth, of not being profligate with its treasures, of—if you will—being a good husband. Today, we speak of recycling, which reflects a part of that attitude, but I think it is important to recover all of the attitude—the thriftiness that seeks out and holds on to what endures, not just what can be reused in some way.

I think of the injunctions I received as a child: "don't leave your bike outside"; "take care of your clothes." Again, there can be many different motivations behind those disciplines, but they are actions that reflect respect. Caring for what is in our possession, making things last. My father used to send us away from the supper table to turn off lights that we had left on. To this day I turn lights off (or feel guilty when I leave them on). I did so before I had much awareness of energy issues, but now it is one habit I don't have to learn.

Respect for creation goes beyond caring and saving and making things last. It includes paying attention to, listening to, and learning from nonhuman others as well as human ones. As I wrote that sentence, one of the cats in our house settled into my lap. Her presence is a concrete reminder that writing something is sometimes easier than practicing it—although in this case writing something is also harder to do, with a cat lying on my arm!

Respect for other creatures includes appreciation and knowledge of plants and other animals for what they are, not simply for what they can provide. They are priceless treasures, not just resources. It also means consciousness about their welfare as well as our own. It means that the daily decisions I make about my life and habitat are made in relation to the lives and habitats of plants and other animals. I think of them, for instance, as I consider running an errand in the car today or waiting until the day after tomorrow, when I have to go out anyway. Wolves, weeds, and spiders become part of the company of "significant others" that shape my day-to-day existence.

Although white women have not had much economic power, we do have, along with women and men of color and indeed many white men, significant economic responsibility, and we can take power. We shop, we hold jobs in and outside the home, we travel, we play. All of those activities involve us in the economic systems in which we live. We also do an enormous amount of economic activity that is ignored by those who talk and write about economics: we bake pies for the church supper; we take a casserole over to a family in which someone has died; we exchange babysitting services; we knit a sweater for a nephew's Christmas present; we pick up the neighbor's children along with our own after soccer practice; we volunteer at the local food bank; we give rides to those who are reluctant to drive alone at night; we work on voter registration; we lobby the state legislature and write our congresspeople; and on and on and on. Whether we work for cash income or not, we also perform a wide range of unpaid (in money) activities. And together, our paid work, our purchasing and exchanging for money, and our unpaid work add up to a very significant economic role, one in which we can exercise power.

And it is in this economic realm—which so pervades each minute of our days and nights, pervades in different ways the ecosocial locations of all of us—that we should increasingly reflect the excellence of respect. Preserving the habitat of the spotted owl and, closer to home, cleaning up Casco Bay are fine and commendable activities. I have no wish or intention to minimize those commitments, although there is a need for ongoing discussion about what actions are appropriate. Here I simply want to emphasize, to lift up, and to focus on a specific sphere—economic life—as a critical context for excellence. Respect for the whole of creation—human and other—sends me directly to economics.

Much of the rest of this chapter explores our lives as post-Christendom Christians in the economic structures. Before I move to that discussion, however, I want to return to the question I raised in relation to courage: how might we nurture respect? The answer is similar to the answer given above for courage: the church can and should support respect for the whole of creation wherever respect is found, modeling it and involving members in deepening it through study, worship, and action.

The church nurtures respect by preaching an ethic of love that includes oneself and the rest of creation. Christian love may lead to self-sacrifice, but it is far from equal to self-sacrifice. It is interesting to me that so much of the traditional discussion of love has focused on its identity as Christian and on the distinctions among *agape, philia,* and *eros.* But Jesus' story of the rich young man turns on the question of who the neighbor is, not on the nature of love. I am sure that the young man would have willingly sold all that he had in order to help his family, but giving it to the poor was more than he could accept.

Christian love takes its shape from Jesus' proclamation of the coming realm, the new creation, the new society; it broadens our understanding of our neighbor. It does not mean that we are not to include ourselves in that understanding. God loves us too. We are our nearest neighbor.

Women—white middle-class women, battered women, raped women, women sexually abused as children, all women—need to hear that message. We are loved by the heart of the universe. We need to hear it concretely—in music, sermons, study, and prayers that name us—not necessarily as individuals but as *women*. We need to hear it in stories of women who have claimed it for themselves.

We also need space and support for anger. I expect many of us need to be able to be angry at God—at a God who, we have been told, uses violence against us to punish us or who somehow, inscrutably, uses violence against us to further God's own will. Part of providing this space and support includes providing safety and confidentiality for sharing our stories. Little is more powerful, educational, and ultimately healing than sharing one's own story and hearing the stories of others. Muriel Ruckeyser once wrote, "If one woman told the truth about her life, the world would split open." I believe it does split open, and each time a new seed of justice and healing emerges.

Learning to respect ourselves and other women also includes acknowledging our heritage for what it is—patriarchal and violent. I still get angry when the Genesis Sodom story is trotted out in defense of anti-gay attitudes and everyone ignores Lot's offer of rape! We can't whitewash the past; it has shaped us in its ugliness as well as its beauty. It also should provide resources for helping women understand the present, understand the structural as well as the interpersonal sources of low self-esteem and violence against us. It can offer women a feminist social analysis.

The church thus can provide space and support for personal, theological, and social exploration. Such work complements what nonchurch groups can offer women, for example, a battered women's group or a consciousness-raising group or a therapeutic group. If such groups do not exist, however, then the church should initiate opportunities for them.

The church nurtures respect also by modeling it. I consider myself extremely fortunate to have had women in my life who loved themselves as well as others. The church desperately needs, throughout its congregations, women who hold positions of leadership and who model respect for themselves, for other people, and for the rest of creation.

The church nurtures respect for others and the rest of creation in ways similar to how it nurtures self-respect—through study, worship, action, and modeling. Anti-racism education, as well as education on other forms of oppression, must be an intrinsic part of the post-Christendom church. UCC churches must become "open and affirming," that is, must be publicly on record that they welcome gay and lesbian people, if they are to model respect (and courage).

As we engage in anti-racism work, it is difficult not to begin feeling guilty. Understanding what is needed concretely to respect others—in the ways we think about creation and institutionalized patterns of policy and action—can feed into negative and destructive themes within our own white psyches. Such work, therefore, must enable white women to see how we are connected to other patterns of violence and discrimination, both as victimized by it and as privileged by it, so that women can understand that we did not set these patterns up that way, that we have some power as well as responsibility to help change them, *and* that in working for change, we also improve our own lives.

So courage and respect are two qualities for the white church and white women to nurture. I may still be afraid, but I speak anyway. In turn, courage nurtures respect. As I speak out, I gain self-respect. At the same time, I can work on extending and deepening respect for the whole of creation, and this will nurture the courage to speak and take risks. And as I take a few steps of courage and respect, I will find new dimensions of healing from the wounds of life in this society, will become a participant in the work of justice—and will gain deeper and deeper insight into what it means to be faithful to the call of Jesus and to live in reliance on the spirit of God.

ECONOMIC LIFE

Along with many others seeking more just economic systems, I work on three fronts: resisting the constant threat and all too often the actuality of an increasing gap between rich and poor; opposing the ever-more-pervasive reach of transnational corporations; and founding an alternative structure in the rich soil of local communities and regions, supplemented and enhanced by wider, including international, partnerships. I have had at times to add a fourth front—fighting for daily survival—although that has not been a constant struggle for me.

Obviously, much—too much—of the time and energy of people on the margins is spent on the fourth and the first fronts, on surviving and resisting. In Maine, these people are primarily women and children, although men are certainly represented. They are primarily white, although people of color are certainly represented, particularly indigenous people. In the past few years, many of us have organized simply to try to stem the tide of cuts at the federal and state levels, cuts initiated by the Republican contract with the rich. In Maine, we were relatively successful in preventing some of the most punitive measures from being adopted.

This kind of effort continues to be essential. Help in procuring food, shelter, clothing, education, and medical care has to be made available; and it should be made available in ways that respect the people forced to receive it. But help is not welfare or benefits, and it is a long way from justice. One of the first things we should do, and Wilma Scott Heidi suggested this thirty years ago, is name such help accurately. She coined the phrase "survival assistance." I propose we adopt the phrase.

Survival assistance was originally seen as a transitional measure, and it still is, although it often becomes a permanent feature of a family's life. But it is designed to be a safety net or assistance until the adult can find a job and support his/her family. Last year, much of the debate in Maine focused on the kind of job necessary and the kind of educational assistance and length of other assistance to be provided until such a job could be found. A major problem in Maine is that jobs paying enough to support a mother and two children are not readily available. This is due in part to regions in the state where jobs don't exist and in part to a continuing double standard in pay and in jobs generally filled by women.

This is clearly a serious weakness in survival assistance legislation. There is, however, an even more serious one, which I hear very little debate about: the assumption that "the poor" can and should be brought into the current capitalist system. More "liberal" assistance programs assume that the poor can become part of a middle class; more "conservative" programs assume they can become part of a working poor if they really try. In the struggle to help people survive, in other words, we end up supporting the status quo.

I find this true also of many "alternative" efforts to improve the economic situation of people in Maine. A number of organizations have been established over the past fifteen years to support women's businesses or to help women start small businesses, for instance. These groups are in fact quite effective, but there is little critical systemic economic analysis. The assumption seems to be that women need help moving into the system—or, rather, holding our own on the margins of it.

My own analysis, as well as that of many feminists and others committed to justice, is that there is so much that is unethical about the current economic system— global capitalism—that we must pursue an alternative one. Before sketching how such an alternative might work, however, I want to frame the discussion within the image of kindom and the three principles of sustainability, justice, and well-being.

FRAMEWORK
Kindom. In the discussion of God and creation, I mentioned the images of kin and household as ways of seeing the world and as a context for thinking about economic life. I want to reaffirm those images here. What happens when we think of the global economy as a household economy, as a way of meeting the economic needs and well-being of relatives? This is, after all, the linguistic root of the word "economy." When I say that forests and rivers and Asian women, men, and children are my kin, I see

them differently from the way I do when I say that they are resources for a lumber company or are an untapped (and cheap) labor force for a shoe company.

For Christians, the forests, rivers, and Asian people are kin. We are all potential friends, sisters, and brothers loved by a God who yearns that we come to love one another. As we think about economic justice, therefore, we need—in order to *see* one another—lenses other than the traditional capitalist or even some of the socialist ones. We need lenses, images, and metaphors that help us see our relatedness as kin as more basic and more important than our relatedness as workers, laborers, managers, and raw materials. These are roles and components of our relationality. Roles are necessary, but they can and should change as needed to support and enhance human and biotic community.

So we are kin, most of us broken within ourselves and apart from one another, but kin nevertheless. The task of economic justice is to discern together how to arrange the production, distribution, and consumption of goods and services for the household. The principles of sustainability, justice, and well-being offer further guidance for our arranging.

Sustainability. A cluster of more specific principles help to spell out sustainability. They include the following: the earth is not ours; we must maintain diversity of life; and life on the planet should continue after us. The earth and its people are God's, created in beauty and diversity, capable of awesome power, rich in life and sure in death. A few people should not own or be able to make life-and-death decisions routinely about either the earth or its people.

Further, both physical and social diversity should be celebrated and nurtured. Physical diversity increases and enriches the genetic pool, and a more varied genetic pool allows for the development of species and individuals that are strong and that can adapt to changing conditions. Physical diversity seems also to enhance the survival and growth of ecosystems, which become less vulnerable to storms or droughts.

Socially and physically, diversity enriches our cultural, ethical, and spiritual life. Different cultural heritages contribute a wide variety of arts, political, and economic resources and spiritual insights to inform, challenge, and delight our humanity. Plant and animal (including human) diversity offers an abundance of opportunities for communication, learning, celebration, and response to God. And as we acknowledge our relatedness to more and more creatures, our own lives expand and grow beyond any horizon we can now imagine.

And finally, as human beings, but more specifically as white Western human groups and individuals, we should not leave the earth the worse off from our presence. Land, water, and air, as well as plant and animal inhabitants, should endure and/or be able to be renewed. We must use only what can be replenished naturally or use only when there is enough to continue indefinitely, so far as we can anticipate. We simply have no right to continue the destructive pattern of species extinction, exhaustion of nonrenewable resources, pollution of air and water, and impoverishment or destruction of most of the world's people and the land. Such behavior is blasphemy.

Justice. The economically relevant principles of justice include the following: we should have the power to shape our lives, including our work lives, in concert with others; we should all share equally in the responsibilities and benefits of our work; and our decisions should be set in a larger context than this town, this state, this region, or this country. These principles, in connection with those of sustainability, mean that as much of our economic activity as possible should be done locally *and* that decisions about local self-sufficiency must be made in relation to the needs and resources of other communities. An emphasis on a more local economy need not and should not lead to an isolationism. These principles also mean that both the political and the economic decision-making structures should be democratic. This, in turn, means a real shift in power away from international arenas to local ones and away from a hierarchical management structure to a grassroots—worker and recipient—structure.

Further, if all are to share equally, work must be totally desegregated and every provision made for all to participate as they can. Child care must be available and/or workers must be allowed to work at home, but again without isolating people.

Well-Being. The relevant principles here are sufficiency (enough to live well) and time and opportunity (enough to develop a whole range of individual and communal interests and skills and to address a similar range of needs and aspirations). Species and individuals should have enough food, appropriate shelter and clothing, safety, health, opportunities for education, creative expression and enjoyment, nurturing relationships, and communication.

Sufficiency includes being able to make some choices, not being forced to live at a minimalist level. It includes having quality resources that nurture the body-spirit, for example, beauty and sensuousness: it mandates an economy that encourages one to enjoy the feel of a piece of wood or to delight in the colors of cloth.

For nonhuman creatures, such sufficiency includes the freedom to live in one's natural habitat and relationships. It includes being able, in any way that makes sense to them, to enjoy one another, one's own food and drink, one's companion, and one's own skin, fur, or shell.

Well-being also includes opportunities for creativity, education, and travel—expanding one's horizons, growing emotionally and spiritually as well as physically, maturing, and then dying. Again, for nonhuman creatures, sufficiency includes the growth of the spirit and creativity in whatever ways are relevant. This principle means that we must have the time to study, play, pray, and make love as well as work. What we now call work—or jobs—should occupy much less of our day and evening time than it currently does.

VISION

My vision focuses on Maine, which is where I live. It recognizes, however, that Maine is part of a global pattern. My vision has been developed in conversation with many others, across the barriers of gender, race, class, sexuality, age, and ability. It has been developed in alliance.

My vision of Maine is rooted in strong regional and local economic structures. They enable all of us not only to survive but to live well—with food that is nourishing as well as enjoyable, with shelters and clothes that are warm in the winter and refreshing in the summer. Maine is blessed with a climate and soil that can provide this range of support. We can harvest a wide range of vegetables, fruits, nuts, berries, meat, seafood, fowl, dairy products, wheat, sugar (from sugar beets), and herbs. So far as I know, we don't naturally grow coffee, citrus fruit, spices, or cotton. But we can produce wool, linen, and leather. We have sun, wind, wood, rivers, and tides for energy. We have wood, straw, stone, and clay for building materials and housing items. We do not have the raw materials to manufacture steel, tin, aluminum, or plastics, although we should be able to make plastics from plants. One of the great resources in Maine is hemp. And hemp is an important source for paper. We must find a way to be able to cultivate hemp and reduce the assault on trees!

Making a good life for all from these resources is the work of all. For instance, we will lovingly make fewer things to last and even to pass on to others. We can make most things locally. We make what we need with love and creativity and then stop. If we have resources that we can use to produce goods that another community needs, or resources that another community can use, we will share them.

Doing this work ourselves dramatically reduces the use of highways and the need for truck transports and warehouses. In turn, we dramatically reduce the use of fossil fuels, nonrenewable resources, and plastics and the release of toxic emissions. We then free up some road-maintenance funds for education and other purposes.

In Maine, a more community-centered economy is as possible for urban areas as it is for more rural ones. With some creative planning, nearly every neighborhood area in Portland, the state's largest city, could become more food- and shelter-sufficient by reclaiming land for community gardens, using rooftops for gardens, planting fruit and nut trees, putting parts of lawns into gardens, and renovating houses and commercial buildings. Each neighborhood could also plan for and help fund a diversity of energy sources and could upgrade energy efficiency through a variety of means. It is not too soon to explore the possibilities of neighborhood-based solar and wind sources for energy. Portland rooftops have ample exposure to both wind and sun. Add a community craft-and-learning center, a fresh-produce market, and a recycled clothing and furniture center, and the neighborhood becomes a mini-village with its own life and vitality.

I envision that communities or neighborhoods, not individual homeowners, will erect solar panels or windmills or whatever. I understand that this can be done more efficiently on a somewhat larger scale, lessening the amount of material resources and ensuring that everyone has access to the heat, light, and electricity that is provided.

Further, I envision that this economy will combine bartering, communal sharing, and money. These forms of exchange characterize both the local economy and the trade and sharing with other communities. We can exchange lobsters for coffee, or blueberries for oranges, as well as pay for them in currency.

Economic practices that do not include money or include it only minimally have a long tradition in Maine and elsewhere. A fishing person I know once commented: "It is a way of life in Maine. I got my boat through bartering." This system is what some economists call the "informal economy." The Finnish feminist economist Hilkka Pietilä names it the "free economy," since it includes the work we do for free.[4] Pietilä estimates that 54 percent of economic activity in Finland falls within the free economy; if paid for, it would be worth 35 percent of the monetary value of the whole economy. I don't know current figures for the United States, but I do much as a volunteer—washing dishes, writing up minutes of a meeting, counseling, and teaching an adult-education class. All of these activities are part of the free economy. What I am proposing is acknowledging and formally institutionalizing this dimension of the economy, which is generally ignored.

Communities can put together many combinations of sharing, trading, bartering, and cash. For instance, in my area, excess from gardens can be brought to a central place and made available for free to those who do not have space for a garden. Or proceeds can be exchanged for help in a neighbor's garden. Money will be needed to complement or supplement what can be shared, traded, or bartered.

Central to the workability of these proposals is the establishment of a community center or the neighborhood centers mentioned above. There should be a multipurpose place where people can meet and just sit and talk if they want, where local produce can be sold, traded, bartered, or shared, where farmers and others from outlying areas can bring their goods and receive from what is there, where craftspeople can bring their wares, where classes can be held, where clothing, furniture, household items, farm and garden items, toys, and books can be recycled. Concerts, art exhibits, poetry readings, and dramas could be scheduled here. This place could also include a day-care center. People could volunteer, barter, or trade staffing time for goods and services. As much as possible, the center should be within walking or wheelchair distance of many townspeople. Bike racks and some form of public transportation should also be available.

Such centers are important for the efficient and equitable distribution of resources. A staff person and computer could keep track of bartering or other exchanges. If the decision has been made that each household is entitled to a bushel of apples if it wants that many, someone could ensure that everyone, including those who may be homebound, receives what they want.

But the centers would also be important for helping to maintain an interpersonal sense of community. Most people of the town would cycle in and out, perhaps many times during a week; they would greet each other and come to recognize names and faces. Many would share the responsibilities of staffing the centers, across the racial and other lines that currently separate us. Such a center institutionalizes our relationality.

It also offers residents an abundance without having to own so much. If I want something new to wear to a party, for instance, I could go to the center and find an outfit free or for some exchange. After the party, I would clean it and return it, making it available for someone else.

Produce and other items could be placed in large containers, and people could bring reusable containers to fill from the large ones, similar to what many natural-food stores and co-ops already have. And the concept—and reality—of trash would eventually vanish from our vocabulary and the land.

Work would not be organized hierarchically. The community works; the community makes "managerial" decisions; the community shares in the results. The community may empower temporary groups or task forces to do research on a topic for decision and to carry out decisions, but these are temporary groups, and the power base remains with the community—the town or village. In the few large cities of Maine, many of those decisions can be made in neighborhoods. Only those decisions that really cannot be made at a grassroots site will be made by representatives of larger units—a city, the towns along a river. I envision that the welfare of birds and deer and corn and pine trees and children (a person over the age of fifteen will be considered an adult in every way) will be represented at those decision-making councils.

As I indicated above, no jobs are segregated in any way. If there is work that no one wants to do, that work will be shared equally, perhaps on a rotating basis. Otherwise, individuals are encouraged to follow their interests and skills.

What has traditionally been called "work," that is, paid employment, as well as the activities that have not historically been considered "work" (much of women's work, for instance)—the services and the production of goods necessary for a secure and healthy society—will require only about the equivalent of twenty hours a week. My reading of indigenous societies is that members spent much less time than we do at "work," perhaps the equivalent of about five hours a day.

What might we do with the rest of the day and evening? Some time will be spent in politics—making decisions about our life together—but much can be spent inventing, playing, talking with seals, making love, creating art, riding bikes, enjoying one another, dreaming, and sharing our lives and wisdom.

With an equal power base and equal access to resources, all the diversities that exist here and elsewhere will be celebrated and learned about informally and in educational and cultural institutions. And we will create new rituals to mourn our different but tragically related pasts as well as to celebrate them and to anticipate a more creative future together.

In this future of God's and the world's, families will be as diverse as members need and create. They will range from one person to many; some will cross several generations and include different combinations of the gender of adults and children. A range of ceremonies witnessing to commitments and separations will exist; and families will live within the larger arms of local communities and the earth. Again, because of the respect and celebration of such diversity and an equal economic arrangement, choices about family configurations will not result in less income or in discrimination.

The Maine I envision will be much healthier than now and will need less medical care and less costly medical insurance. We will all have nutritional food organically grown, less stress, more time to nurture mature and caring relationships (which will come from many different members of the community, not just one's immediate family), less pollution, more economic security, and I believe, less violence. Our immune system should be strengthened, and the environmental and emotional sources of ill health will be reduced. The emphasis will be on prevention, and healing will emphasize restoration to self and community as well as a range of technologies and procedures that will stay as close to natural processes as possible. The economic support of more sophisticated and expensive medical technology will be clustered in regional research-teaching hospitals available by air or land ambulance service and in outpatient resources available through the computer and by local practitioners representing a wide range of technical skills and healing wisdom.

FROM HERE TO THERE

Obviously, much of what is involved in moving from where we are now to our visions of a more just future, a society that is at least open to God's future, to new creation, is resolve. The move does not require technological breakthroughs, a total collapse of the status quo, or a revolution. Many of the activities I have envisioned for the future are already being done now, particularly in the "informal" or "free" economy. The congregation I envisioned in chapter 1 was also implementing dimensions of this future. If we as a church and/or as a people can move from being victims of "market forces" to agents and can recognize that economic life, like any other part of life, has been constructed and can be reconstructed in light of shared beliefs and values, we can make great strides toward a more just future. Groups of people can get together and decide to "do" economic life differently. We don't need major changes in federal or state legislation to take many of the necessary steps.

Since I have imagined some of these steps in the chapter on the church, my focus here will be on some of the legislation that might facilitate such a transition. In particular, I wish to address how to provide both a floor and a ceiling on income, as well as a shared economic security.

I find both property taxes and sales taxes to be unfair in Maine. Property taxes prevent many Mainers from living in the communities where they grew up, particularly coastal communities. Being able to live by the ocean should not be the prerogative of the rich but a matter of community planning. Similarly, sales taxes unequally burden people who are poor.

Instead, I propose that the state of Maine provide a basic income for each household—an income that is available to everyone and that ensures access to health care, decent housing, and post-high-school education as desired. I recognize that this will need significant federal help, and much of the following discussion can be applied to the federal level. My focus is on Maine primarily to suggest ways of proceeding.

A basic income can be funded through income tax credits, supplementary cash payments made monthly, vouchers, and even some community service, for example, participating in neighborhood watches, working in community gardens, or staffing community centers. The ration books of World War II, present-day food stamps, and the coupons I had in college to use in the cafeteria are all forms of vouchers that we are familiar with. I propose vouchers for perhaps half of the basic income, since they can most easily serve as the transition to the bartering and sharing part of the economy. Vouchers can be used for a significant portion of food, clothing, heat and energy, and some health care, for instance. The point is that however the basic income is funded, it is available to everyone. We all have the same access to fundamental resources.

This basic income must be realistic. If an income of $24,000 a year in Maine (based on 1994 figures) is necessary for a minimally *sufficient* life for a household of one adult and two children, the basic income should provide a significant portion or all of it.[5]

There are good reasons for either option, for providing only some or all, but I think I prefer the latter. Guaranteeing all that is necessary provides the most security, eliminates any double standard, and is not subject to the shifts in the economy that affect jobs and pay. But I don't know if this option is really feasible. Further, it does seem to me that some shared work in the community is extremely valuable. So I propose guaranteeing half of what is necessary.

In addition to a guaranteed basic income through some combination of money, vouchers, and activity, a more just tax policy should be enacted. It would emphasize a graduated income tax and an investment tax, supplemented by a business income tax and a qualified property tax. For the personal income tax, income up to the cost of living would be tax-free. Then a steeply graduated tax would be placed on income up to $300,000. After that, income is taxed 100%. The figures would vary some-what according to household size and/or dependents. But there should be a limit. Does any family really need more than a total of $300,000, particularly when most services such as insurance and education are included in what is guaranteed for all? Even that figure strikes me as obscene.

Income taxes, however, address only part of the redistribution. For many today, including people in Maine, the principal of extremely rich investment portfolios is not touched. We must put an upper limit on wealth. Above, I suggested $300,000 as the point at which income is taxed 100%. Perhaps the best way to make unearned wealth available for redistribution is to limit the amount that can be inherited to $300,000. Any amount over that goes to the state for redistribution directly to citizens, with a percentage made available to education and local services, for example, fire, public transportation, and supplementary police—supplementary to citizen policing.

Business and corporate taxes can then also be addressed. Since in my proposals there will eventually be less need for the state to attract businesses and for large corporations to provide a number of jobs, profits can be taxed in a steeply graduated way with fewer loopholes. Rigorous legislation and community expectations about how businesses conduct themselves regarding the products they make or services they render, the earth, and the people who work for and/or with them should help to weed out unsustainable and insensitive businesses and should gradually help to diminish the need for too many nonlocal ones.

Finally, I suggest a qualified property tax. Residences, particularly second residences, could be taxed, but not the land. This policy would enable people of modest means to live near the coast and in the mountains. It would also enable the state and communities to tax summer residents who are "from away" and who take advantage of local services.

If I know that my family, friends, and I have basic economic security, a number of results can begin to follow. I do not have to work twelve hours a day or commute to Portland, which adds another ten hours a week to my work-week. I can work if I want to, or I can cut back to part-time. My life becomes a little less hectic, and my blood pressure may even go down! I have time to write, to follow my activist heart, and to participate in the further redirection of the local economy. Working part-time enables someone else to have part-time work, and two part-time employees require less financial outlay from my employers, in my case the Maine College of Art, than one full-time person. The college can breathe a little sigh of relief or put that money into scholarships or much-needed library acquisitions. In other words, a different economic spiral gets started that can benefit myself and many others.

With changes in taxes and the resultant redistribution of income, changes in the federal, state, and even local bureaucracies can occur. Less money and fewer people would be needed to ensure that people who still might fall through cracks—primarily children—have the resources they need for a good life. The punitive and humiliating constraints of so much of survival assistance legislation should disappear. The number of its workers should decrease. The power of that bureaucracy over its "clients" should end. There will still need to be some of this assistance, but I propose that it be concentrated locally and supervised by those currently most marginal to the dominant society. Decisions about survival assistance should be made by grassroots organizations and by the peers of those needing some survival assistance. The federal government should play a back-up monitoring role and develop broad guidelines, but the specifics should be flexible so that the local community can relate them appropriately to its own situation and, perhaps more important, so that it can have ownership of them. If the local communities can, to some significant extent, write their own specific legislation, they have power and will not feel (and indeed will not be) imposed on by people "from away" who know little about life in Maine.

A percentage of the money from a steeply graduated income tax, from inheritance taxes, and from the savings due to a much smaller welfare bureaucracy can then be returned to local communities to help start small, ecologically responsible, community-based businesses. These incentives will begin to replace the current tax breaks and other incentives that Maine offers to attract businesses and corporations "from away." Although it may be important to continue to attract some of these businesses because of what they offer in terms of quality of life or necessary goods or services, a major effort can also be put toward encouraging homegrown businesses.

As I indicated above, since everyone will have a basic income, these businesses will not need to hire full-time workers and thus can spread out the number of jobs available. People who want to earn more can work more than one job or can go into business for themselves and work as much as they want and/or as much as others utilize what they have to offer. At the same time, of course, legislation will be necessary to ensure that a business is sustainable, and a steeply graduated income tax will help set limits.

A reduction in the amount of time that people must work for income would considerably ease the child-care crisis in this country. Child-care centers would certainly be included in the businesses and could be connected with places of work. At the same time, parents would have more time to spend with their children, and other family members and friends would be able to share the responsibilities and joys of being with children. And special legislation could be passed to raise the basic income for parents who want to spend the first year or so at home with a new child.

All of these are modest proposals. I think they are all "doable." There are also dimensions that I have ignored—education for one, particularly work-related education. I think that there would actually be more money and volunteer or bartered efforts to support creative educational programs than there is now. And more important, with education, as with jobs, people would decide what kind of training they need or want, in light of the future they want to see. It would no longer be a matter of trying to "keep up" with the faceless "theys" who determine what kind of jobs are necessary and what kind of education is appropriate for those jobs.

By way of concluding this chapter, I want to address briefly the relationship of the alternative economy I am proposing to the current global economy and to a range of injustices and violence. My proposals offer a war of attrition on international corporations and large businesses in general. There is currently no international political agency to monitor or legislate international corporate practices. Some concerned people have proposed a code of ethics for these corporations and businesses, but my cynical streak makes me skeptical of both how rigorous such a code would be and the extent to which it would be enforced. Boycotting and similar tactics have some effect, but they would be significantly strengthened if corporations found that they were becoming redundant. If I (and thousands of others) could buy a pair of shoes locally and even individually made, or could barter for them rather than buy a pair from Reebok, Reebok eventually must curtail its business. It might choose to leave Thailand, and perhaps that country becomes freer to redirect its own economy rather than be swept up in one that is unsustainable for it as well as for the earth in general. Assistance may still be necessary for Thailand, but it too would change. Rather than provide loans to build a factory for Reebok, assistance could be given to farmers to provide food for their own people, not cash crops for Westerners.

Further, one of the consequences of my proposals is that people will need less cash income. This may allow some U.S. corporations to stay at home rather than go abroad where labor is cheaper and ecological restrictions are less rigorous. At home, they can help increase the job possibilities, and it is easier to tax and monitor them. (Ideally, I envision their disappearance, but I recognize that this is both ideal and ultimate.)

Third, in place of Reebok's providing jobs for Thais, a citizen's organization in Maine may enter into a trading relationship with one in Thailand to exchange rice for blueberries. So far as the Maine co-op is concerned, of course, the blueberries designated for exchange are those over and above what is needed to satisfy Maine appetites and are grown with minimal or no artificial fertilizers or pesticides. If they are being cultivated (as opposed to growing wild), such use of the land will have been determined by a local group in light of the area's overall land needs and ecological appropriateness.

Fourth, with respect to the global economy, all kinds of communication, including travel, will still exist, but without Thailand being swept into more and more service industry jobs, which tend to be minimal in pay and stereotyping. There will be some business travel; professional people will gather for conferences and exchanges. And with somewhat more leisure time, people in general may choose to travel to Thailand. Money earned beyond the cost of living can be put toward travel, for instance; equally, travel becomes more available to a wider range of people. I hope that the net result of all this will actually be a reduction in the volume of travel and an increase in the diversity of who travels, thus also reducing the pressure on the airways as well as decreasing the energy consumption and the use of nonrenewable resources.

Finally, what are some of the connections between my proposals for an alternative economy and other expressions of oppression? All forms of oppression must be addressed specifically and the connections made among them. Here I can, however, sketch some of the ways in which addressing economic and class issues affects some of the others.

The alternative economic structure I am proposing most obviously challenges classism and issues of power. By redistributing income and making access to resources more equal, we reduce hierarchies of power and gatekeeping (an elite that determines who gets what and when). Further, grounding the new structure locally further redistributes power, making it available to all who are willing to participate, if not directly, certainly in a more genuinely representative manner. Power is more equally distributed across groups in all the social locations of a community or region—racial-cultural, age, sexual orientation, ability, religion, and class.

This equalization of power and the emphasis on working together to shape the future and to solve problems certainly form one of the most important dimensions of justice, as I have described elsewhere. Power—agency—is central to living, at least in the West. This is true not only of human beings but also of the rest of creation, as we understand it. Power is essential to our spirits as well as our bodies. As people are more able to exercise power, they are less likely to remain victims, and those who seek to dominate are more likely to be challenged.

The new economy helps challenge a major dominant assumption that perpetuates gender and racial oppression: that men are "providers" and work outside the home while women are homemakers and caretakers. This isn't often true, but the cultural legacy is often an obstacle—for middle-class white women homemakers in battering situations, for instance, and for women whose husbands have died or left them. And this assumption has been a source of conflict and oppression for the poor, particularly African American poor; women have often been able to secure jobs as domestics, whereas men have remained unemployed. My proposals put economic power into the hands of all, women and men of all groups and ages. Gender identities will have to be based on something other than provision of income and jobs.

Finally, my proposals should reduce the need for abortions insofar as economic factors influence a decision about abortion. The inability to provide for another child, for instance, should no longer be a critical consideration. Decisions about population size still have to be made, but that discussion belongs to a different context.

The above are proposals for Maine. I think they would work over a long period of time, but they could be started now. Some such changes are already occurring. As "doable" changes are made, they lead to others until gradually, but intentionally, a whole new edifice is built. Nevertheless, they are proposals. There may be—and I am sure there are—other ways to accomplish the same or similar goals. Certainly what groups in New York or Boston can and should do will in some areas be quite different from what I propose to be done here in Maine. But my underlying point is that we should be laying the groundwork for an alternative economic structure— one that is more humane, ecologically responsible, sustainable, and just. The specifics of how that will take place should vary from place to place.

In conclusion, we can both critique and begin to reorganize the economy in light of the principles I have articulated. In so doing, we can move toward a more just and sustainable economic order. Such a new order will in turn facilitate movements toward racial and gender justice and will help liberate the world's people and the earth from the colonialism of Western global economics. Ethicist Carol Robb has written, "Only when women achieve economic justice will sexual justice be possible."[6] I agree but would add that economic justice is essential for all people and the earth. Equally, racial justice, ecological justice, and all other forms of justice are essential if we are to achieve economic justice.

The congregation I envisioned in chapter 1 began to understand this interrelation of structures. It also began to recognize both that action on one structure leads to change in others and that action must take place on all structures. It is not sufficient to focus only on structures that shape economics or gender or racial patterns or sexual orientation or abilities or age. These must all be addressed in light of their interdependence even as a specific congregation may spend more time and energy on one or two of them. Beacon Street Congregation encouraged ongoing consciousness-raising and analysis on issues of race, class, and gender. It also was able to bring the perspectives of gay and lesbian people, of old and young people, and of people with disabilities to bear on worship, community life, and discipleship. At the time of this writing, it was developing an extended commitment to economic challenge and transformation in the state and in its own locale. Programs included a dental and medical clinic, an organic garden with shared work and produce, and a plan to make affordable housing available to very poor people in the community. A community bartering system was being developed.

These are all activities that any congregation can do. They are examples of activities that a congregation should do. The specifics will vary, depending on an analysis of need and structure, on the location of the congregation, and on what else is occurring positively or negatively.

The impact of such activity can be tremendously increased if congregations join together, both within a denomination and across ecumenical lines. If members of five churches came together to determine legislative priorities and positions and then lobbied for them and developed any of the programs illustrated by Beacon Street, the result could be miraculous. I am not at all underestimating the stubbornness of centuries-old structures, but I am deeply aware that, at least in Maine, we have not begun to develop our own local alliances for justice. There is so much that we can do. We need neither money nor experts. We need only a basic understanding of the gospel and its relation to contemporary patterns of social power, the will to act, and a willingness to be open to the wind of the Spirit.

The theology and ethics I have developed have been born out of my own struggles with oppression and unearned privilege, my love of God and commitment to justice, the incredibly rich voices of people engaged in similar struggles, and the ache and anger in my heart at the beauty and desecration of this earth and its inhabitants. I do not have much confidence that significant global change will occur without an intervening major catastrophe. I do know that we have to continue. I do know that we must live not only in resistance to the status quo but also in anticipation of new creation.

As feminists, we are variously connected to congregations, some of us much more tenuously than others. Our needs and responsibilities will differ depending on these connections. Some of us may still be struggling to be included in the language of worship or to create a space in which we have a voice. Some of us have other communities of support and inspiration to sustain us as we labor in our traditional religious communities. Others of us will be able to speak and even exercise some leadership in our churches.

Whatever our situation, it is important to honor our own needs, yearnings, and limits. If we are to be faithful, we must also be nourished. So we do what we can and must in our own situations. I pray that we all can allow others to reach out to us and that we can reach out to others, joining together in our own ongoing creation and in that of the world.

I look out my window and inside myself and see a beautiful, fragile, and tormented world. Our hearts are created to delight in all that God has made, to work with God to care tenderly for all whose hearts and bodies are broken, to resist the forces that break us, to welcome healing, and to celebrate the birth of each new plant that heralds the breathtaking promise of new creation.

Behold! I make all things new.

NOTES

INTRODUCTION: COMMITMENTS TO SHARE AND ACT

1. Rachel Henderlite was a southern, white, Presbyterian minister and teacher. She taught "Christian Ethics" at the Presbyterian School of Christian Education in Richmond. In her courses, she introduced me to many of the ideas I am now developing theologically. In the 1950s, she became a member of All Souls Presbyterian Church in Richmond and was one of the very few white members in that congregation. She was the first woman to be ordained in the Presbyterian Church, U.S.A. She was an incredibly gracious, courageous, and demanding woman. She is one of our heroes, whose legacy has helped me reclaim my own Christian and white female heritage.

2. Peggy McIntosh, "White Privilege and Male Privilege: A Personal Account of Coming to See Correspondences through Work in Women's Studies," working paper 189, Wellesley College Center for Research on Women, Wellesley, Mass., 1988.

3. Delores Williams, *Sisters in the Wilderness: The Challenge of Womanist God-Talk* (Maryknoll, N.Y.: Orbis, 1993), 185.

4. See, for instance, *Time,* April 4, 1993, 46, and Loren B. Mead, *Transforming Congregations for the Future* (Bethesda, Md.: Alban Institute, 1994), 16.

5. As *feminist* comes out of a primarily white women's heritage, *womanist* comes out of African American women's history. Originally identified by Alice Walker, womanist theology is described by Delores Williams as "a theological corrective . . . bringing black women's experience into theology so that black women will see the need to transform the sexist character of the churches and their theology." It is "a prophetic voice reminding African-American denominational churches of their mission to seek justice and voice for . . . the entire African-American community, female and male, adults and children." Williams, *Sisters in the Wilderness,* xiii–xiv.

6. Quoted in Beth Blissman, "Toward a Vision of Earth Community: Theological Reflections on the Role of Euro-Americans" (unpublished paper, Iliff School of Theology, Denver, Colorado).

7. Williams, *Sisters in the Wilderness,* 203.

8. Delores Williams, "Womanist/Feminist Dialogue: Problems and Possibilities," *Journal of Feminist Studies of Religion* 5, no. 9 (spring/fall 1993): 73.

9. Although my focus is on economic issues, I cannot urge congregations too strongly to address these in relation to racism and other structures of oppression. Two resources for such exploration are *America's Original Sin: A Study Guide on White Racism,* by the editors of *Sojourners* (2401 15th St. NW, Washington DC 20009), and my manual on addressing racism in *Ending Racism in the Church,* edited by Susan Davies and Sister Paul Teresa Hennessee (Cleveland, Ohio: United Church Press, 1998).

10. Williams, *Sisters in the Wilderness,* and Susan Brooks Thistlethwaite, *Sex, Race, and God: Christian Feminism in Black and White* (New York: Crossroad, 1989).

1. COMMUNITIES OF RESISTANCE AND NURTURE

1. *Time,* April 4, 1993.
2. Mead, *Transforming Congregations.*
3. Richard Quebedeaux, *The Worldly Evangelicals* (San Francisco: Harper and Row, 1978), 72. Quebedeaux suggests that the typical evangelical male is white, has a $150,000 home and two cars, is a businessman or professional, has a wife at home, and is head of the home.
4. Sidney Blumenthal, "Christian Soldiers," *New Yorker,* July 18, 1994, 32.
5. "Christian Coalition Congressional Scorecard" (1994 Election Edition, Chesapeake, Va.).
6. Blumenthal, "Christian Soldiers," 36.
7. Ibid.
8. Quoted in Harvey Cox, "The Warring Visions of the Religious Right," *Atlantic Monthly,* November 1995, 68.
9. Ibid.
10. *Christian Century,* February 16, 1983, 140.
11. Ibid.
12. *Faith and Freedom: Reforming the Church's Social and Political Witness* 15, no. 3 (winter 1995–96).
13. Quoted in Conference Steering Committee, "Newsletter" (n.d.), 1.
14. Ibid.
15. Communicated in a presentation at the American Academy of Religion Conference, November 18, 1995.
16. IRD, "A Call to Women of the Church" (Washington, D.C.: Institute for Religion and Democracy, n.d.).
17. Ibid.
18. "Goddesses of Their Own Choosing," *Faith and Freedom,* 7.
19. What follows is one possible response. There are many other reponses that can lead a congregation to deepened faith, a vocation of justice-action, and witness to new creation.
20. Williams, *Sisters in the Wilderness,* 167.
21. For an initial discussion about how some of this consciousness-raising might occur, see Beverly Harrison, "Toward a Christian Feminist Liberation Hermeneutic for Demystifying Class Reality in Local Congregations," in *Beyond Clericalism: The Congregation as a Focus for Theological Reflection,* ed. Joseph Hough Jr. and Barbara Wheeler (Atlanta: Scholars Press, 1988), 137–51.

2. METHODS OF CONVERSATION AND COMMITMENT

1. Williams, "Womanist/Feminist Dialogue," 71.
2. Ibid., 73.
3. Luise Shottroff, *Lydia's Impatient Sisters: A Feminist Social History of Early Christianity,* trans. Barbara and Martin Rumscheidt (Louisville: Westminster John Knox Press, 1995), 8.
4. Judith Plaskow, with Toinette M. Eugene, Ada María-Díaz, and Kwok Pui-lan, "Appropriation and Reciprocity in Womanist/Mujerista/Feminist Work," *Journal of Feminist Studies of Religion* 8, no. 2 (fall 1992): 107.

5. Williams, *Sisters in the Wilderness.*

6. Plaskow et al., "Appropriation and Reciprocity," 108.

7. Toni Morrison, *Beloved* (New York: Penguin, 1988).

8. Carol Christ, "Why Women Need the Goddess: Phenomenological, Psychological, and Political Reflections," in *Womanspirit Rising: A Feminist Reader in Religion,* ed. Carol P. Christ and Judith Plaskow (San Francisco: Harper & Row, 1979), 273–87.

9. Valerie A. Abrahamsen, *Women and Worship at Philippi: Diana/Artemis and Other Cults in the Early Christian Era* (Portland, Maine: Astarte Shell Press, 1995), 46.

10. Ibid., 129–50.

3. THEOLOGY OF GOD AND THE WORLD

1. Martin Buber, *I and Thou,* 2d ed., trans. Ronald Gregor Smith (New York: Charles Scribner's Sons, 1958), 75.

2. H. Richard Niebuhr, *The Responsible Self: An Essay in Christian Moral Philosophy* (New York: Harper & Row, 1963), 123.

3. Carol Gilligan, *In a Different Voice* (Cambridge: Harvard University Press, 1982).

4. H. Richard Niebuhr, *The Meaning of Revelation* (New York: Macmillan, 1962), 189–90.

5. Hannah Arendt, *On Violence* (New York: Harcourt, Brace and World, 1969), 42.

6. Thistlethwaite, *Sex, Race, and God,* 121.

7. Elizabeth A. Johnson, *She Who Is: The Mystery of God in Feminist Discourse* (New York: Crossroad, 1993), 249.

8. Thistlethwaite, *Sex, Race, and God,* 121.

9. Carter Heyward, *Touching Our Strength: The Erotic as Power and the Love of God* (San Francisco: HarperSanFrancisco, 1989), 188.

10. Ibid.

11. Emilie M. Townes, *Womanist Justice, Womanist Hope* (Atlanta: Scholars Press, 1993).

12. Ibid., 195.

13. Ibid., 194.

14. Williams, *Sisters in the Wilderness,* 150.

15. Ibid., 22.

16. At that time Harding was a journalist as well as an activist for racial justice. He recalled this experience in an article about the civil rights movement, but I don't remember the journal in which I read the article.

17. Johnson, *She Who Is.*

18. Ibid., 255.

19. It is also true, of course, that for some people, such images are very important because their own family relationships were so bad. As one woman said to me the other day: "I was abused by my father, and I don't consider him a father. God is my father."

20. Although the traditional Christian spelling is "Yahweh," I am using the spelling that, as I understand it, respects the orthodox Jewish position of not calling on God by name.

21. Abrahamsen, *Women and Worship at Philippi,* 129–50.

4. ETHICS OF CREATION AND NEW CREATION

1. Katie Cannon, *Black Womanist Ethics* (Atlanta: Scholars Press, 1988), 32.
2. Alice Walker, *In Search of Our Mothers' Gardens: Womanist Prose* (San Diego: Harcourt Brace Jovanovich Publishers, 1983), 232–33.
3. Margaret Walker, *Jubilee* (Boston: Bantam, 1966).
4. Edward J. Pennick, "Land Ownership and Black Economic Development," *Black Scholar,* January–March 1990, 44.
5. Theodore Rosengarten, *All God's Dangers: The Life of Nate Shaw* (New York: Alfred A. Knopf, 1974).
6. For an extended discussion of this approach to land and value, see John Locke, *Second Treatise of Civil Government* (Buffalo: Prometheus Books, 1986).
7. Pennick, "Land Ownership and Black Economic Development," 43.
8. Ibid.
9. Emilie M. Townes, *In a Blaze of Glory: Womanist Spirituality as Social Witness* (Nashville: Abingdon Press, 1995), 55.
10. Ibid., 56.
11. Williams, *Sisters in the Wilderness,* 117.
12. Rosengarten, *All God's Dangers,* 530–31.
13. Robert Coles, *Migrants, Sharecroppers, Mountaineers: Children of Crisis,* vol. 2 (Boston: Little, Brown and Co., 1967), 180.
14. Ibid., 187.
15. Ibid.
16. Ibid., 188.
17. Barbara Christian, *Black Feminist Criticism: Perspectives on Black Women Writers* (New York: Pergamon Press, 1985).
18. Walker, *In Search of Our Mothers' Gardens,* 241.
19. Morrison, *Beloved,* 88.
20. Alice Walker, *Living by the Word* (San Diego: Harcourt Brace Jovanovich, 1988).
21. Lorraine Anderson, ed., *Sisters of the Earth: Women's Prose and Poetry about Nature* (New York: Vintage, 1991), v.
22. Susan Griffin, *Woman and Nature: The Roaring Inside Her* (New York: Harper and Row, 1978), 1.
23. Joan Parrish, unpublished notes, made available to me personally.
24. Jeffrey P. Bain et al., *Clues to America's Past* (Washington, D.C.: National Geographic Society, 1976), 16.
25. Annie Dillard, *Pilgrim at Tinker Creek* (New York: Bantam, 1974), 8.
26. Gregg Easterbrook, *A Moment on the Earth: The Coming Age of Environmental Optimism* (New York: Viking Press, 1995), 671.
27. Cited in Easterbrook, *A Moment on the Earth.*
28. Murray Bookchin, *Remaking Society: Pathways to a Green Future* (Boston: South End Press, 1990), 33.
29. Based on what I have read about the history of the earth, however, other events (e.g., ice ages) may have had more impact on the earth than did human decisions.

30. The phrase, as I remember it, is Martin Buber's.

31. Quoted in Vera L. Norwood, "Heroines of Nature: Four Women Respond to the American Landscape," *Environmental Review* 8, no. 1 (spring 1984): 45.

32. I can no longer find the source of this story.

33. Evelyn Fox Keller, *A Feeling for the Organism: The Life and Work of Barbara McClintock* (New York: W. H. Freeman and Co., 1983), 198.

34. Ibid., 199.

35. Ibid., 194–95.

36. Donald Worster, *Nature's Economy: A History of Ecological Ideas* (Cambridge: Cambridge University Press, 1977), 165.

37. Carolyn Merchant, *Ecological Revolutions: Nature, Gender, and Science in New England* (Chapel Hill: University of North Carolina Press, 1989), 256.

38. Williams, *Sisters in the Wilderness,* 167.

39. Ibid., 166.

40. Kelly Brown Douglas, *The Black Christ* (Maryknoll, N.Y.: Orbis, 1994), 108.

41. Jacquelyn Grant, *White Women's Christ and Black Women's Jesus: Feminist Christology and Womanist Response* (Atlanta: Scholar's Press, 1989), 220.

42. Rosemary Radford Ruether, *Sexism and God-Talk* (Boston: Beacon Press, 1983), 138.

43. Rita Nakashima Brock, *Journeys by Heart: A Christology of Erotic Power* (New York: Crossroad, 1991), 69–70.

44. Johnson, *She Who Is,* 163.

45. Ibid., 162.

46. Townes, *In a Blaze of Glory,* 123.

47. Ibid., 140.

48. Ibid., 144.

49. Hannah Arendt still has the best discussion of the meaning and the political significance of forgiveness. See *The Human Condition* (Garden City: Doubleday Anchor, 1959), particularly pages 212–18.

50. Delores Williams, "A Womanist Perspective on Sin," in *A Troubling in My Soul: Womanist Perspectives on Evil and Suffering,* ed. Emilie M. Townes (Maryknoll, N.Y.: Orbis, 1993), 144.

51. "The UN Summit for Social Development," *Global Advocates Bulletin,* no. 29 (June 1995): 2.

52. Hannah Arendt, *Eichmann in Jerusalem: A Report on the Banality of Evil* (New York: Viking Press, 1963).

53. Stephanie Seguino, *Living on the Edge: Women Working and Providing for Families in the Maine Economy, 1979–93* (Orono, Maine: Margaret Chase Smith Center for Public Policy, 1995).

54. Williams, "A Womanist Perspective on Sin," 146.

5. TRANSFORMING LIFE IN THE WORLD

1. M. Shawn Copeland, "Wading through Many Sorrows," in Townes, *A Troubling in My Soul,* 124.

2. Townes, *Womanist Justice, Womanist Hope,* 212.

3. In an excellent article on anger, Beverly Harrison explores the connections between anger and love in much more detail than I have done here. See "The Power of Anger in the Work of

Love: Christian Ethics for Women and Other Strangers," in *Making the Connections: Essays in Feminist Social Ethics,* ed. Carol S. Robb (Boston: Beacon Press, 1985), 2–21.

4. Hilkka Pietilä, *Tomorrow Begins Today* (Helsinki, Finland: n.p., 1985), 9 (paper presented at ICDA/ISIS Workshop in Forum 85, Nairobi, Kenya, July 1985). See also Marilyn Waring, *If Women Counted: A New Feminist Economics* (San Francisco: HarperSanFrancisco, 1988), 300–304.

5. Seguino, *Living on the Edge.*

6. Carol Robb, *Equal Value: An Ethical Approach to Economics and Sex* (Boston: Beacon Press, 1995), 159.

SELECTED BIBLIOGRAPHY

Abrahamsen, Valerie A. *Women and Worship at Philippi: Diana/Artemis and Other Cults in the Early Christian Era*. Portland, Maine: Astarte Shell Press, 1995.

Anderson, Lorraine, ed. *Sisters of the Earth: Women's Prose and Poetry about Nature*. New York: Vintage, 1991.

Arendt, Hannah. *Eichmann in Jerusalem: A Report on the Banality of Evil*. New York: Viking Press, 1963.

———. *The Human Condition*. Garden City: Doubleday Anchor, 1959.

———. *On Violence*. New York: Harcourt, Brace and World, 1969.

Bookchin, Murray. *Remaking Society: Pathways to a Green Future*. Boston: South End Press, 1990.

Brock, Rita Nakashima. *Journeys by Heart: A Christology of Erotic Power*. New York: Crossroad, 1991.

Buber, Martin. *I and Thou*. 2d ed. Translated by Ronald Gregor Smith. New York: Charles Scribner's Sons, 1958.

Cannon, Katie. *Black Womanist Ethics*. Atlanta: Scholars Press, 1988.

Christ, Carol. "Why Women Need the Goddess: Phenomenological, Psychological, and Political Reflections." In *Womanspirit Rising: A Feminist Reader in Religion*, edited by Carol P. Christ and Judith Plaskow, 273–87. San Francisco: Harper & Row, 1979.

Christian, Barbara. *Black Feminist Criticism: Perspectives on Black Women Writers*. New York: Pergamon Press.

Davies, Susan, and Sister Paul Teresa Hennessee, eds. *Ending Racism in the Church*. Cleveland, Ohio: United Church Press, 1998.

Dillard, Annie. *Pilgrim at Tinker Creek*. New York: Bantam, 1974.

Douglas, Kelly Brown. *The Black Christ*. Maryknoll, N.Y.: Orbis, 1994.

Gilligan, Carol. *In a Different Voice*. Cambridge: Harvard University Press, 1982.

Grant, Jacquelyn. *White Women's Christ and Black Women's Jesus: Feminist Christology and Womanist Response*. Atlanta: Scholar's Press, 1989.

Griffin, Susan. *Woman and Nature: The Roaring Inside Her*. New York: Harper and Row, 1978.

Harrison, Beverly. "The Power of Anger in the Work of Love: Christian Ethics for Women and Other Strangers." In *Making the Connections: Essays in Feminist Social Ethics*, edited by Carol S. Robb, 2–21. Boston: Beacon Press, 1985.

———. "Toward a Christian Feminist Liberation Hermeneutic for Demystifying Class Reality in Local Congregations." In *Beyond Clericalism: The Congregation as a Focus for Theological Reflection*, edited by Joseph Hough Jr. and Barbara Wheeler, 137–51. Atlanta: Scholars Press, 1988.

Heyward, Carter. *Touching Our Strength: The Erotic as Power and the Love of God*. San Francisco: HarperSanFrancisco, 1989.

Johnson, Elizabeth A. *She Who Is: The Mystery of God in Feminist Discourse*. New York: Crossroad, 1993.

Keller, Evelyn Fox. *A Feeling for the Organism: The Life and Work of Barbara McClintock.* New York: W. H. Freeman and Co., 1983.

Merchant, Carolyn. *Ecological Revolutions: Nature, Gender, and Science in New England.* Chapel Hill: University of North Carolina Press, 1989.

Morrison, Toni. *Beloved.* New York: Penguin, 1988.

Niebuhr, H. Richard. *The Meaning of Revelation.* New York: Macmillan, 1962.

———. *The Responsible Self: An Essay in Christian Moral Philosophy.* New York: Harper & Row, 1963.

Robb, Carol. *Equal Value: An Ethical Approach to Economics and Sex.* Boston: Beacon Press, 1995.

Rosengarten, Theodore. *All God's Dangers: The Life of Nate Shaw.* New York: Alfred A. Knopf, 1974.

Ruether, Rosemary Radford. *Sexism and God-Talk.* Boston: Beacon Press, 1983.

Seguino, Stephanie. *Living on the Edge: Women Working and Providing for Families in the Maine Economy, 1979–93.* Orono, Maine: Margaret Chase Smith Center for Public Policy, 1995.

Shottroff, Luise. *Lydia's Impatient Sisters: A Feminist Social History of Early Christianity,* translated by Barbara and Martin Rumscheidt. Louisville: Westminster John Knox Press, 1995.

Thistlethwaite, Susan Brooks. *Sex, Race, and God: Christian Feminism in Black and White.* New York: Crossroad, 1989.

Townes, Emilie M. *In a Blaze of Glory: Womanist Spirituality as Social Witness.* Nashville: Abingdon Press, 1995.

———. *Womanist Justice, Womanist Hope.* Atlanta: Scholars Press, 1993.

Walker, Alice. *In Search of Our Mothers' Gardens: Womanist Prose.* San Diego: Harcourt Brace Jovanovich Publishers, 1983.

———. *Living by the Word.* San Diego: Harcourt Brace Jovanovich, 1988.

Walker, Margaret. *Jubilee.* Boston: Bantam, 1966.

Waring, Marilyn. *If Women Counted: A New Feminist Economics.* San Francisco: HarperSanFrancisco, 1988.

Williams, Delores. *Sisters in the Wilderness: The Challenge of Womanist God-Talk.* Maryknoll, N.Y.: Orbis, 1993.

———. "A Womanist Perspective on Sin." In *A Troubling in My Soul: Womanist Perspectives on Evil and Suffering,* edited by Emilie M. Townes. Maryknoll, N.Y.: Orbis, 1993.

Worster, Donald. *Nature's Economy: A History of Ecological Ideas.* Cambridge: Cambridge University Press, 1977.

INDEX

abortion, 129

Abrahamsen, Valerie, 51

access to resources, 45

aesthetic images, 93

alliances, 2, 11–15, 92–93; acting in coherence, 14–15; breaking down walls, 12–13; community in alliance with others, 27–28; congregational alliances, 2, 27–28; making commitments, 11–12; and witness, 33–36

"Am I Blue?" (Walker), 78

anger, 110–12, 116

apocalyptic imagery, 99–100, 101

Arendt, Hannah, 56, 57, 103

Artemis, 51, 69

Asherah, 52

Augustine (Saint), 53, 66

Bacon, Francis, 76

baptism, 31–32

beauty, creation of, out of nature, 77

Beloved (Morrison), 48–49, 77–78

Bible, 41–43, 107

Bookchin, Murray, 85

Bridget, 68–69

Brock, Rita Nakashima, 99

Buber, Martin, 54–55, 62, 64, 111

Cannon, Katie, 47

Carson, Rachel, 89

Center for Vision and Policy, 4, 12

charisma, 44

child care, 127

Children of Crisis (Coles), 77

Christ. See Jesus

Christ, Carol, 50

Christian, Barbara, 77

Christian Coalition, 21

Christian ethics: and Christian presence, 108–17; and decision-making, 106–8

Christian Right, 20–23

church, 8–10; and Christian Right, 20–23; as context, 39; and economy of United States, 23–24; growth of, 20; and Jesus, 99; prophetic heritage of, 23; and respect, 116–17; and secularization, 19–20; women in, 49–50, 51–52. See also community

circle of stones, 52

Coles, Robert, 76–77

Color Purple, The (Walker), 78

commitments, 11–12

communion, 31

community, 18–19, 24–25; in alliance with others, 27–28; becoming community, 28–30; and Christian Right, 20–23; of discipleship, 26; and economic structure of United States, 23–24; moved away from the center, 19–24; and resurrection, 98; role of prophetic heritage, 23; and secularization, 19–20; spiritual life and worship, 30–33; transformation of, 24–30; and witness, 33–36

Cone, James, 57

congregational alliances, 2, 27–28

congregations, as sources for feminist theology and ethics, 8–10

constitutionalists, 21

construction, and response, 82–86

context, 37–39

Copeland, M. Shawn, 109

courage, 110–13

covenant, 92–93; celebration of, 33; of membership, 32

creation: of beauty out of nature, 77; construction and response, 82–86; createdness as value, 94–96; doctrine of, 72–73; historical–social constructions of, 73–82; of humans and other creatures, 86–94; images of, 92–94; as new creation, 1–2, 96–102; and sin, 102–4; and transformation, 105; white feminist construction of, 82–96

creativity, power of, 64–65

culture, 80

Curry, Elinor, 50

Daly, Mary, 57, 83

Darwin, Charles, 85, 91

Davies, Susan, 16

Davis, Angela, 78

decision-making, 106–8

Dillard, Annie, 65, 85

discipleship, 26

dominance, 7

dominion theology, 21, 88

Douglas, Kelly Brown, 99

ecological justice, 1–2, 11, 45–46, 72–73. *See also* creation

economics, 75–76, 102–3, 115, 117–31; alternative economy, 121–31; economic structure of United States, 23–24; global economy, 128–29; income redistribution, 125–28; and justice, 120; and kindom, 118–19; and sustainability, 119–20; and well-being, 120

ecosocial location, 5–8, 37–39

Ecumenical Coalition on Women and Society, 22

education, 127–29

Ellison, Marvin, 16

equinox celebration, 33

ethics, 55; ethic of responsiveness, 54–55; and

feminist theology, 2; relational approach to, 107–8; and theological method, 43–46. *See also* Christian ethics

evangelicals, 20–23

Faith and Freedom, 22

farming, 75–77

fecundity, 93

Feminist Spiritual Community, 4

feminist theology and ethics, 2; congregations as sources for, 8–10; feminist reimaging and reconstruction of God, 57–67; justice as source for, 10–11; men's experience as source for, 41; women's experience as source for, 39–41. *See also* theological method

forgiveness, 63

gender, and God, 67–71

Genesis Community Loan Fund, 4

Gilligan, Carol, 55

global economy, 128–29

God: as enemy, 62; experience of, 40, 56; feminist reimaging and reconstruction of, 57–67; and gender, 67–71; images for, 67–71; Jesus as image of, 70–71; kinship of, 92; as male, 51; names of, 67–71; as object of loyalty and love, 66–67; power of, 57–58; power of creativity, 64–65; power of liberation, 61–62; power of mutuality, 62–64; power of mystery, 65; power of solidarity, 60–61; power of survival, 59–60; as radically monotheistic, 55–56; and relationality, 54; as relational power, 58–66

goddess traditions, 22–23, 50–52

Good News, 22

Grant, Jacquelyn, 99

Griffin, Susan, 79–80

Gustafson, James, 66

Hagar, 47, 58

Hall, David, 16

Haney, Eleanor, 2–5

Harding, Vincent, 62
Harrison, Beverly, 106
hatred, 110–12
healing, 33, 43
heart, 86, 89
Heidi, Wilma Scott, 118
Henderlite, Rachel, 3, 50, 54
Heyward, Carter, 57, 62–63
homophobia, 84
hooks, bell, 39
household, 92
human commonality, 86–94
humans, and other creatures, 86–94

images: aesthetic, 93; apocalyptic,
    99–100, 101; of creation, 92–94;
    feminist reimaging and reconstruction
    of God, 57–67; for God, 67–71; Jesus
    as image of God, 70–71
In a Different Voice (Gilligan), 55
incarnation, 51
inclusive language, 31
income redistribution, 125–28
infant baptism, 31–32
Institute for Religion and Democracy (IRD),
    21–23
international corporations, 128–29
Isaiah, 1, 18, 68

Jesus, 26, 31; apocalyptic images of, 99–100,
    101; and the Bible, 41–43; and the church,
    99; death of, 97–98; as image of God,
    70–71; ministry of, 58; and new creation,
    96–100; resurrection of, 98, 100–101; as
    social reality, 99
Johnson, Elizabeth, 57, 67–68, 99
justice, 44–46; defined, 10; ecological, 1–2,
    11, 45–46, 72–73; and economics, 120;
    social, 1–2, 11; as source for feminist
    theology and ethics, 10–11

Keller, Evelyn Fox, 90
kindom/kinship, 92, 118–19

land use and ownership, 74–77
Leighton, Debbie, 16
liberation, 61–62, 92
Lilly, John, 90
Lorde, Audre, 37, 47, 57, 62–63
Luke, 72
Luther, Martin, 60

man, historical–social constructions of,
    73–82
Margulis, Lynn, 85
McCallum, Brigit, 53
McClintock, Barbara, 90
McDonald, Jay, 58
McIntosh, Peggy, 6
Mead, Loren, 20
membership, covenant of, 32
men's experience, as source for feminist
    theology, 41
Methodist church, 22
monotheism, 55–56
Morrison, Toni, 48, 77–78
mutuality, 62–64
mystery, 65

names of God, 67–71
National Council of Churches, 22
nature: creation of beauty, out of nature, 77;
    historical–social constructions of, 73–82;
    natural world, 11, 61, 63–64, 72–73, 85,
    86–94. *See also* creation
new creation, 1–2, 96–102
Niebuhr, H. Richard, 54–56, 62, 66

obedience, 55
On Violence (Arendt), 56

Paul, 92, 98–99
Peck, Scott, 20
Pennick, Edward J., 74
Pentecost, 100–101
personal power, 44
Pietilä, Hilkka, 122

Plaskow, Judith, 47, 48
Plato, 109
power: of creativity, 64–65; distribution of, 40; of God, 57–58; of liberation, 61–62; of mutuality, 62–64; of mystery, 65; personal, 44; redistribution of, 129; relational power of God, 58–66; social, 44–45; of solidarity, 59–60, 60–61; of survival, 59–60; types of, 44–45
Presbyterian church, 22
Presbyterian Laymen, 22
property tax, 126
prophetic heritage, 23

quality of life, 46

radical monotheism, 55–56
redemption, 1–2
Re-Imagining Conference, 22
relationality, 54–55, 107–8
relational power, God as, 58–66
religions, in theological method, 46–52
Republican Party, 20–21
resources, access to, 45
respect, 113–17
response, and construction, 82–86
Responsible Self, The (Niebuhr), 54–55
responsiveness, ethic of, 54–55
resurrection, 98, 100–101
revelation, 54
Rich, Adrienne, 1
Robb, Carol, 130
Robertson, Pat, 21
Ruckeyser, Muriel, 116
Ruether, Rosemary, 99
Rushdoony, Rousas John, 21
Russell, Letty, 41
Russell, Valerie, 50

sacraments, 31–32
salvation, 1–2, 100
Sarah, 47
Savell, Susan, 18

Sea Around Us, The (Carson), 89
seasonal rituals, 33
secularization, 19–20
self-respect, 113
Sex, Race, and God (Thistlethwaite), 16
Shaw, Nate, 74–75, 76
She Who Is (Johnson), 67
Shottroff, Luise, 42
sin, 102–4
Sisters in the Wilderness (Williams), 16, 97, 113
Sisters of the Earth, 79
social justice, 1–2, 11
social power, 44–45
solidarity, 60–61
solstice celebration, 33
Sophia, 67
spiritual life, and worship, 30–33
suffering, 57
sufficiency, 120
survival, 59–60
survival assistance, 118
sustainability, 45–46, 119–20

taxation, 125–27
theological method, 37; the Bible and Jesus, 41–43; and circle of stones, 52; context and condition, 37–39; and ethics, 43–46; role of different traditions in construction of, 46–52; and women's experience, 39–41
theology construction, 53; affirming dimensions of the past, 53–56; feminist reimaging and reconstruction of God, 57–67; and gender of God, 67–71; God as object of loyalty and love, 66–67; God as relational power, 58–66; and images of God, 67–71; and names of God, 67–71
Thistlethwaite, Susan, 16, 37, 57
Thoreau, Henry David, 91
Tinker, George, 12
Townes, Emilie, 57, 75, 99–100, 101, 109
traditions, in theological construction, 46–52

transformation, 106; and Christian presence, 108–17; of community, 24–30; and creation, 105; and decision-making, 106–8; and economics, 117–31

United Church of Christ, 20
United Voice, 4

value, 94–96
virtue, 108–9

Walker, Alice, 47, 73–74, 77–78
Walker, Margaret, 74
well-being, 46, 120
Wells-Barnett, Ida, 109
white middle-class Christian feminist theology and ethics, 1

Williams, Delores, 8, 14–15, 16, 22, 26, 38, 47, 58, 76, 81, 97, 102, 103, 113
WINGS (Women in Nurturing Group Support), 4
witness, 33–36
Woman and Nature (Griffin), 79–80
womanist, 47
Womanist Justice, Womanist Hope (Townes), 57
women: in the church, 49–50, 51–52; historical-social constructions of woman, 73–82; women's experience, as source for feminist theology, 39–41
worship, 10, 29, 30–33
Worster, Donald, 91